MW00816792

Praise for
Mystic Secrets Revealed

"The power to change ourselves is quite potent. Edwin Harkness Spina's *Mystic Secrets Revealed* is a guide to inner transformation ..."
—*Midwest Book Review*

"*Mystic Secrets Revealed* rises above many spirituality and personal growth books due to its absorbing anecdotes, exactness, humor, and short, realistic key applications."
—*Mindquest Review of Books*

"I'm very impressed ... I've studied metaphysics all my life and I feel like a beginner. Thank you for your splendid work."
—Glenna Citron, Culver City, CA

"That is by far the best explanation I have ever read on consciousness and awareness ... Thank you for sharing."
—Ken Hall, Yukon, OK

"Wow! If you want to step out of fear, anger, depression and step into joy, happiness and bliss, this book is the book you will want to read. Ed Spina clearly and simply opens your consciousness; he awakens you to a new understanding of how to create better realities in our own lives."
—Cindy Parkinson, Vancouver Island, Canada

"I got my hands on many other books which all helped me on my journey. But for some reason, your book has done for me what none of those others could. It's made me feel alive again and that life is worth living." —Shirley Carolan, Oceanside, CA

"The guidance of a master, who gives his counseling from his own experience and understanding. This makes this book especially authentic." —Beata Levai, Székesfehérvár, Hungary

Mystic Secrets Revealed

Revealed

53 Keys to Spiritual Growth and Personal Development

Edwin Harkness Spina

Copyright ©2011, 2019 Edwin Harkness Spina

All rights reserved under International and Pan-American Copyright Conventions. No part of this text may be reproduced, transmitted, downloaded, decompiled, reverse engineered, or stored in or introduced into any information storage and retrieval system, in any form or by any means, whether electronic or mechanical, now known or hereinafter invented, without the prior express permission of the author, except for brief quotes used in reviews.

ISBN: 978-0-9745871-9-6

Cover photo: Rainbow on the Tibetan Plateau
                    by Edwin Harkness Spina
Published by Higher Dimensions Publishing, Inc.
Printed in USA

MysticWarrior.us
EnergyCenterClearing.com

Table of Contents

Table of Contents (con't)

Acknowledgments

It would be a book in itself to properly acknowledge all my family, friends, colleagues, co-workers and antagonists who contributed, directly and indirectly, to the lessons contained in *Mystic Secrets Revealed*.

Mystic Secrets Revealed was written over the course of six years, during which time I traveled extensively throughout North America, South America and Asia, and interacted with thousands of people. Many contributed greatly by "setting the stage" upon which the various mystic principles revealed themselves, both at work and at play.

Those individuals who I would like to acknowledge personally are: Tommy Rosa, who contributed immensely to my energetic expansion of consciousness; my original mentor, "Sophie," who opened me up to a world I never knew existed; and my editor, Willy Mathes, who, in addition to being a great editor, always provided wise counsel whenever I needed it.

Thank you all.

—Edwin Harkness Spina

Introduction

Many of us become so wrapped up in our careers, relationships and other day-to-day affairs, that we forget what is most important to our overall well-being. We fail to remember the popular adage, "We are spiritual beings living a human existence." The trials and tribulations of the physical world are *intended* to stimulate us to evolve our consciousness, connect with our innermost self, and ultimately achieve mastery. The expression of the unique gifts we each discover to be our own inevitably leads us to peace and joy. This is the true mission of our "soul."

I, too, found myself guilty of this oversight. In my case, I had started several new companies, each of which was regularly beset with crises that consumed all my energy and attention. When things would go well, I had no time. When things went poorly, I had no money. At one point, I was flat broke, without a car, being evicted from my apartment, my girlfriend breaking up with me, and my company going out of business. This dramatic fluctuation in my fortunes forced me to contemplate, "What's the point?"

Following my intuition, I began to study—both in books and with advanced spiritual teachers—the timeless, universal principles that manifest all reality. After developing a solid understanding of these principles, I wrote my first book, a novel, *Mystic Warrior*, which described a world where selfless mystics were using advanced spiritual skills to influence world events and prevent a nuclear catastrophe.

Mystic Warrior was very well received, winning the *Independent Publisher's Book Award for Visionary Fiction*, a *Nautilus Silver Book Award for Fiction*, and receiving outstanding reviews and testimonials. When many readers wrote asking, "How do I do this?", I began to compile my thoughts.

Many of my reflections found their way into my monthly *Mystic Warrior Newsletter*, which eventually became the basis for *Mystic Secrets Revealed*.

Mystic Secrets Revealed is a short, yet potent, spiritual guide, which explains in a clear and direct manner, how you can apply mystic principles to achieve your own, most heartfelt dreams, and attain a life of peace and joy. It's written in concise, bite-sized chapters, many of which are illustrated with colorful, personal examples that can be absorbed in 15 minutes or less.

Mystic Secrets Revealed was written over six years, during which time I got to travel extensively throughout the US, as well as to Peru, Hong Kong, Beijing, Taiwan, Tibet, and Bali. The people I encountered and interacted with set the stage for the mystic principles to reveal themselves, leading to greater understanding and appreciation for our "world" and to a sense of peace and well-being I would not have anticipated prior to my journeys.

If you are like any of the millions of people, just like me, who would like to "escape the matrix," then I encourage you to read *Mystic Secrets Revealed*. Mastering the principles con-tained in this book will help you to attain the peace and joy you've always sought!

1

Mental Alchemy

Back in the Middle Ages alchemists sought to transform base metal into gold. Mental alchemy is the process of transmuting your thoughts to improve your life and expand your mind.

Back in the Middle Ages, alchemists sought to transform base metal into gold. They searched for an elusive substance, the philosopher's stone, which would bring about this conversion or transformation, known as alchemy. But to initiates of the ancient mystery schools, alchemy was primarily an allegory for the real work of spiritual and mental alchemy.

Spiritual alchemy is the process of transforming a less evolved soul personality into a more refined one. Just as a caterpillar can transform into a butterfly, a person struggling through their earthly existence can transform into one who lives in enlightenment, illumination, pure Being, or oneness with the Divine. Spiritual alchemy takes one from a life lived in ignorance, attachment and suffering to a life lived in transcendent knowledge, freedom and bliss.

The founders of all major religions have attempted to expedite this transformation by providing rules or methods to help people achieve this "realized state," and to lead happier and more productive lives. Mystics from all traditions, as well, have studied the universal laws to speed up this process, which many believe occurs over numerous lifetimes.

Mental alchemy is the process of transmuting your thoughts to improve your life and expand your mind. The good news is that this discipline can produce immediate, beneficial results in your current life, in some cases instantly!

Mental alchemy involves the replacement of beliefs that are hindering your development with positive ones that will help

1

you. You might say that sounds straightforward—why would this be so difficult?

It turns out that it's extremely difficult to change beliefs. There are three reasons for this:

1) Most people mistake their beliefs for the truth. Even if it's not in their best interest, some people resign themselves to their fate, because they mistakenly accept a belief as true, and therefore fixed.

2) Beliefs operate at the subconscious level. Most people are unaware of their subconscious beliefs, which are often in conflict with their conscious thoughts. For example, a woman may consciously be seeking to manifest a healthy love relationship, but subconsciously she may feel that she's unworthy. Unless her belief is made conscious and transmuted, it will continue to sabotage her efforts. (This will be covered in chapter 3, *How to Identify Unconscious Beliefs*.)

3) You see what you believe. Less than 100 years ago, physicists were trying to determine whether light was a wave or a particle. They discovered that the answer depended on what you believed you would find. If you believed light was made of particles, then you could design an experiment that proved it. Conversely, if you believed light consisted of waves, then you could design another experiment to prove that.

The placebo effect provides another example. In drug trials required to gain FDA approval, 40% of patients, on average, will obtain relief from placebos. They get better simply because they **believe** they will get better. Placebos have actually helped people with Parkinson's disease.

The mystic principle behind these results is called the Law of Attraction or "like attracts like." In the mystic world, and now in the world of quantum physics, we know that everything is energy. Everything has its own vibration, including a belief. People attract to themselves those experiences that match their existing belief system. They literally get to see what they believe.

So if beliefs are so hard to change, how does Mental Alchemy work?

Neurologists tell us that the brain doesn't know the difference between what's actually experienced and what you *imagine* you're experiencing. The same electrical patterns are fired between the neurons in the brain for both. The electrical patterns in the brain reflect how we store and process information, including beliefs.

The ramification of this is profound: you can change your beliefs using your imagination. It doesn't matter whether the belief is true or not.

Let's take an example of a basketball player who misses the final shot of the state championship game, and his team ends up losing by one point. This experience can be traumatic, and will often reinforce negative beliefs that he's a choker or a loser. Had he made the shot, he obviously would be a hero and filled with the confidence of a winner.

Let's say you are the basketball player. What should you do?

First, go to a quiet place where you won't be disturbed for 10–15 minutes. Make sure that none of your objective senses (sight, hearing, smell, touch, taste) is being stimulated. Take a few deep breaths. Your goal is to relax and get into an "alpha" state. This is a relaxed state in between your normal waking consciousness and sleep, where you feel calm, alert and centered. Scientists have shown that you can learn new skills much more readily while in this state. Meditation is ideal for this.

At this point, you should replay the end of the basketball game in your mind. Only this time, when you take the final shot, do it with confidence and watch it go in. Visualize all the fans going wild, as the buzzer sounds and your teammates carry you off the court. Involve all your senses and imagine how it feels to be the hero!

Michael Jordan is arguably the greatest basketball player of all time, but he probably missed just as many shots at the end of the game as he made. But you can be quite certain he didn't dwell on the missed shots; rather, he learned, probably quite early on, to simply remember and visualize the game-winning shots. You can do the same. Use the technique of Mental Alchemy and change your life for the better, starting today!

2

3 Steps to Manifesting Your Ideal Life

The Law of Attraction specifies that you will attract to yourself those experiences that match your beliefs. Use these mystic principles to manifest your ideal life.

Over the past several weeks, I've received dozens of email solicitations for books, CDs and videos that promise to reveal newly discovered techniques to improve my life. These emails promise a wide variety of benefits: how to get rich, lose weight, meet the woman of my dreams and buy a million dollar mansion with no money down. In some cases, the salesman will throw in a "Ginzu knife" or "pocket fisherman" if I order im-mediately!

While some of these marketers may actually believe they have invented a whole new system of creating a life anyone would want, the truth is "there is nothing new under the sun." Mystics have studied the underlying principles that manifest reality for centuries. These same principles existed in the time of Socrates, and they existed before the establishment of many of today's religions.

Whether it's money, love, health, or anything else, the principles of manifesting such are the same. In mystical terms, the Law of Attraction specifies that you will attract to yourself those experiences that match your beliefs. In the words of quantum physics, "the observer affects that which is observed." Since you are the observer, it's *you* who affects your life; that is, it's *you* who creates your experience of reality!

You create your experience via your underlying beliefs— whether they are conscious or unconscious. If you're not conscious of your beliefs, then you must make them conscious. As Carl Jung said, "Until you make the unconscious conscious, it will direct your life and you will call it fate." Or, as mystics have urged throughout the millennia, *"Know thyself."* This includes your beliefs.

Before you begin to manifest your ideal life, you must get clear on exactly what you want. Examine each of your desires from a mystic perspective. Is it a purely selfish desire, or is it something that could be of benefit to others, as well? If you are attempting to manifest your desire at the expense of someone else, there will be a steep price to pay at some point in the future. Remember, "As ye sow, so shall ye reap;" so why saddle yourself with additional burdens? If your desire seems selfish, reframe it so that it's of benefit to others.

Once you are clear on exactly what you want, then it is a straightforward matter to manifest your desire. There are three steps:

Step 1. Visualize exactly what you want for 5 minutes per day. Let's say you want to go sightseeing in Paris. You may want to visualize the Eiffel Tower. Why 5 minutes? Because any longer and your mind will wander. Any shorter and you may not be fully fleshing out your vision.

Step 2. Put yourself in the picture, with detail and emotion. In your mind's eye, you now have a clear view of the Eiffel Tower. Keep in mind, though, if you don't visualize yourself in the picture, the universe will manifest your desire, but perhaps not in the way you anticipated. For example, you might get a postcard of the Paris skyline in the mail! To avoid any misunderstandings, picture yourself standing in front of the tower. What are you wearing? Are you there with your spouse or some new love interest? Add details, employing all of your sensory data. You're eating a delicious croissant. The wind is blowing gently on a beautiful, sunny spring afternoon. You hear conversations "en français" and you smell the perfume of the "petite jeune fille" standing near you.

Don't forget to add emotion. Are you enjoying the taste of your croissant? Do you feel the joy of exploring a new country? Are you reveling in your newfound sense of freedom as you travel the world? The more realistic you make it, the better.

Step 3. At this stage, focus only on the end result. This is very important! Don't worry or even concern yourself about how you'll get there. You can't possibly imagine *all* the ways that your goal might manifest; so don't limit yourself to people you know or the most obvious avenues to attain your goal. Let the universe take care of the details!

When you are done with your meditation, release it to the universe; that is, just let it go, knowing that it will manifest. Continuing to hold it in your mind will prevent its mani-festation. A wise farmer, once having planted seed in his field, doesn't go out the next day and dig up the seed to see if it's growing yet. You have to *let go,* and trust that the universal laws of nature are using your "empowered intention" to orchestrate the highest good. To ensure you've let go, occupy yourself with a completely unrelated activity after you complete your meditation.

You're ready to go, but first, a brief note of caution. This is an extremely powerful technique, so keep in mind the old adage, "Be careful what you wish for—you just might get it." As an example, an acquaintance of mine was remarking on how lucky a friend of hers was to receive a $100,000 settlement for a personal injury she suffered. Within two weeks, my friend was involved in a moderately serious auto accident that left her with a bad back and a subsequent $50,000 settlement. Was it worth it? I don't think so.

To ensure that you don't manifest something similar, I recommend you close each meditation by saying, "If it be God's Will, then so be it," or "If this is for my highest good, then so be it." This is an extra form of protection that will help you avoid needless headache.

Lastly, don't think that because you're busy visualizing, you don't have to take any action on the physical plane. Taking action is important because it let's the Universe know you made a decision and that you're serious! For example, if you're looking for a boyfriend or girlfriend, you can't just sit inside and visualize your ideal mate; you still need to get out and meet people. Just go about your business, but be alert to opportunities that the universe is presenting to you.

The Law of Attraction is the basic underlying principle at work here. If you're not manifesting what you desire, then there are two possibilities: you aren't clear on exactly what you want or you're not aware of a certain belief, probably unconscious, that is contradicting your conscious desire.

Identifying your unconscious beliefs is a topic that we'll cover in our next chapter.

Until then, manifest your dreams the mystic's way!

3

How to Identify Unconscious Beliefs

In manifesting your ideal life, it is critical to identify and overcome any unconscious, limiting beliefs that might sabotage your efforts.

"Know thyself."

These words were inscribed in the vestibule of the Temple of Apollo at Delphi.

For centuries, petitioners seeking advice from the Oracle at Delphi would view the inscription. Philosophers throughout the ages offered this same advice to their students. These words are as valuable today as they were almost three thousand years ago.

Part of knowing yourself is understanding your beliefs. The difficulty is that most beliefs are subconscious. They have been accepted without ever having been critically examined.

As was described in *3 Steps to Manifesting Your Ideal Life*, the Law of Attraction states that you will attract to yourself those experiences that match your beliefs. These beliefs create your experience of reality. What if these beliefs are in opposition to what you're actually trying to accomplish? What if they no longer serve you? Wouldn't it be useful to identify these limiting beliefs and replace them with beliefs that affirm you are divine, immortal, transcendent, limitless and capable of fulfilling your most heartfelt dreams and highest aspirations?

There are a number of techniques to identify unconscious beliefs: taking a battery of psychological tests or tapping into your inner wisdom via meditation are two approaches you can use. There is a shortcut, however, that can predict with 99% accuracy what your beliefs are. It is so simple that people usually overlook it. Even when it is clearly stated, they frequently ignore it.

After all, most people have accepted their beliefs as true, and don't want to hear anything that might contradict what they believe is true, especially if these beliefs are long held. Remember, however, you are *not* your beliefs. You are a divine spiritual being! So why hold onto anything that is preventing you from realizing this truth?

So here's the secret.

Look around. Whenever you have a repeating problem in some area of your life, then *that* is where you have a false or limiting belief. This doesn't mean that just because you're in between relationships or jobs, you necessarily have a false belief. But if the problem constantly reappears, then you can be 99% certain a false belief is involved.

Avoid the temptation to blame someone for inserting this false belief into your belief system. After all, you could easily point fingers at your parents, teachers, friends, TV, etc., as well as yourself. It's not important where it came from—you just want to be rid of it, so that you can experience your ideal life.

You have two choices here. You can: 1) identify your unconscious beliefs and release them, or 2) learn to recognize the symptoms of accepting any limiting belief and change your thoughts. You can also do a combination of the two.

Choice 1) Use your attitudes to identify your false beliefs. Let's say you want more income, wealth, or abundance. What is your impression of wealthy people? Are you happy for them or resentful? If you're resentful, then what signal do you think you're sending out to the universe? You don't want anything to do with those "rich people!" Consequently, the Law of Attraction states that you won't attract wealth into your life.

One way to free yourself of a negative belief is to write it on a piece of paper and burn it, while telling yourself it is forever banished from your being. Write a positive affirmation on another piece of paper, such as "Good people can have money." And then *use the affirmation*—state it out aloud, while looking in a mirror each day. You can add other affirmations, such as "I am worthy of prosperity" and "Money flows easily to me." Make up your own; there's just one rule, however: you have to phrase it such that you really believe that it's true! That is, you have got to feel it! Repeat whatever affirmation(s) you've chosen aloud 9 times a day for 21 days. This is the length of time it takes to reprogram your instinctive mind, where these beliefs are stored. As the old saying goes: "What you put your attention on grows!"

Choice 2) Make sure you are always sending out the proper vibration. Remember that your goal is make sure that you are sending the right vibration to attract to yourself the experience you desire. The best barometer of whether or not you are sending out the proper signals is to MONITOR YOUR EMOTIONS. If you're not feeling good, then you need to change your thoughts; because the emotions that are being felt indicate your thoughts are sending the wrong message.

Replace your negative thoughts with positive ones. The book, *Ask and It is Given* identifies and ranks 22 emotions. Understanding that most people can't go from hatred to joy in one step, they advise you to simply keep moving up the ladder. Eventually, you'll get to feel joy more and more frequently and for longer periods of time.

In both cases, you have substituted positive thoughts and feelings for negative ones. As was described in our first chapter, mystics call this *Mental Alchemy*, after the old alchemists who transformed lead into gold. You may recognize that this involves a degree of self-observation. As was inscribed on the Temple at Delphi, "Know Thyself."

4

The Surrender of the Ego

A necessary step on the path to enlightenment is the surrender of the ego. When the ego is subjugated to the will of God, you become a spiritual powerhouse.

Almost everyone knows someone who professes to "know everything." These "know-it-alls" are never wrong, seldom accept advice and, once they stake out a position, they will do anything to defend it. At best, they are perfectionists. At worst, they can become delusional, as they fight to avoid being wrong by reinterpreting events that would otherwise cast them in a negative light.

Many people with large egos are reasonably successful. Their followers stroke their egos, which makes them difficult to deal with. When trouble surfaces, the temptation is to sit back, wait for "the fall," and gloat when "he gets what he deserves." But when you come across such an individual, try not to deal too harshly with him. The universe is setting him up for a dramatic lesson that will hopefully propel him forward in his spiritual evolution. His ego is about to be crushed, but once he recovers he will be better off for it.

Recently, I saw this firsthand. Mr. Perfect was a detail oriented businessman who was both unable to delegate and dismissive of advice. He was directing a project that was heading for disaster, but refused all forms of help. At the last minute, he was ordered to accept help. An extremely gifted individual, Mr. Helper, came in at the last minute, but was unable to save the project. Everyone involved commented on the awesome contribution Mr. Helper had made and how lucky Mr. Perfect would be to have him on his team as they moved forward.

Mr. Perfect had a different opinion. Rather than accept any fault for the project's failure, he argued that he would have succeeded if it hadn't been for Mr. Helper. To make matters worse, he issued an ultimatum: either he or Mr. Helper had to go. No one could talk him out of his irrational position. Mr. Helper is now running the project.

Mr. Perfect's desire to be right drove him to "cut off his nose to spite his face." It seemed to trump all logic, including his self-interest.

But from a mystic perspective, this was completely logical and furthermore, ***inevitable***.

Mystics recognize that the subjugation of the ego is a necessary step towards enlightenment. Remember, the goal of a mystic is direct communion with God. As you attune daily with your divine aspect or Master Within, your goal is eventually to align your will with the Will of God. To do this fully, the ego must surrender.

To surrender the ego does not mean that you become a meek, passive doormat who invites abuse. Quite the contrary: when the ego is subjugated to the Will of God, you become a spiritual powerhouse. You become fearless in confronting people in positions of authority, for, in effect, you are now speaking with God's voice.

On the other hand, the ego has no interest in you attaining your full spiritual potential. The ego wants to be in charge. It will create all sorts of rationalizations to keep itself in power and prevent such a shift. It's similar to a politician rationalizing why he supported a bill that was not in his constituents' best interest. "If I don't vote for it, then the next guy will, and then I won't be around to fight for my constituents when a more important issue arises." That's the difference between a politician and a leader.

Surrendering the ego can be even more difficult for someone who has attained a high degree of success in life. The star quarterback, rock star, business mogul or political figure all possess worldly power. They have fans, groupies, shareholders or followers that idolize them.

The biblical adage that it is easier for a camel to go through the eye of a needle than for a rich man to go to heaven, would be equally true if "business mogul," "politician" or "celebrity" were substituted for "rich man." The point is that people who are admired are much more reluctant to surrender the ego than someone with much less to lose.

At the same time, as spiritual beings living a human existence, the Master Within drives all of us to evolve. The eventual surrender of the ego is inevitable. If the conscious mind/ego does not pay attention, the message gets louder. If it is ignored, then eventually, a critical point will be reached and a meltdown will occur.

To avoid a meltdown, consult the Master Within for advice on a daily basis. When your connection becomes strong enough, you will become infused with spiritual power. Rather than a meltdown, others will look to you for guidance; because they will recognize that you speak the Truth.

5

Mysticism, Dogma and Truth

Understanding the universal principles that underlie various religious guidelines can aid in your spiritual evolution and help you avoid getting trapped in dogma.

At a recent lecture on Belief Systems, a student asked, "Is mysticism a religion?"

Mysticism is a spiritual discipline aiming at direct communion with God or the ultimate truth. It is not a religion and, in fact, all religions have mystics. There are Christian mystics, Jewish mystics (Kabbalists), Islamic mystics (Sufis), Buddhist and Hindu mystics. Where all the tenets of these religions intersect is where you'll find the mystics.

Mystics of all traditions also study universal laws, which, by definition, are always true, not merely for a particular era or culture. These truths can be found at the heart of every major religion, and this is why Kabbalists will have more in common with Sufis than they would with their mainstream Jewish counterparts (and vice versa).

In the process of studying and applying these universal laws, a student of mysticism will begin to unveil his or her inner senses. That is, the counterparts of his or her objective senses— sight, hearing, touch, taste and smell—will awaken, which are often referred to as psychic abilities. This is a side benefit, but not the principle goal of mysticism.

After the lecture, someone asked, "Isn't connecting with God the goal of all religions?"

If one is considering religions in their original, purest form, then the answer is yes. But based on the prevailing culture or state of affairs, additional guidelines or conditions are usually tacked onto the universal laws. These rules should be relied upon as *suggestions* meant to improve a person's life, not as universal truths. At best, they are relative truths. As an example, the doctrine of "heaven or hell" is meant to teach that there are consequences to your actions. The universal law underlying this principle is karma, i.e., the law of cause and effect.

Whenever such rules become "the only way," they become dogma. This is true whether we are talking about religion, science or politics. If the letter of the law is rigidly followed without consideration for the spirit of the law, there is the danger of fundamentalist behavior. Understanding the underlying principle would help avoid the possibility of uncontrolled mobs from burning people at the stake.

Picture an extended family getting together for a holiday dinner. The daughter, now married with children of her own, prepares a roast for the evening meal. In the course of her preparation, she cuts off the two ends of the roast, places the roast in the pan and puts it in the oven. Her child asks her why she cut off the ends of the roast. The daughter explains that is how her mother taught her. She then asks her mother, who explains that is how her mother, the grandmother, taught her. Then they ask the grandmother who explains that at the time, her roasting pan wasn't big enough to hold the entire roast, and so she always cut off the ends.

It is not necessary to cut off the ends of a roast to cook a delicious meal. Similarly, the additional rules most religions offer are not necessary to connect with God. Religions play a vital role in encouraging virtuous behavior to the benefit of all; but rigid adherence to these rules *to the exclusion of the main goal of communing with God* is counterproductive and can lead to separation and intolerance. The Golden Rule, "Do unto others as you would have them do unto you," is universally accepted by every major religion. Any action that violates this universal truth inherently breeds conflict, which can ultimately lead to war.

Early on in their training or education, mystics are taught how to attune with God by contacting the Master Within, i.e. the divine aspect at the heart of every individual. The Master Within should be consulted whenever an important decision needs to be made. This is the single best source of direction for anyone. We will cover this in our next chapter.

Imagine God as a bright light covered with various veils. As you peel away these veils, which represent various beliefs and ideas, the light brightens. Your goal should be to connect or commune with this bright light directly. This is your birthright as a spiritual being living on earth. To the mystic, this represents the ultimate goal: illumination.

6

Receiving Direction from the Master Within

*As a fundamental guide about how to act in
every situation, there is no simpler and more elegant
advice than to ask for direction from the Master
Within.*

Recently I had the opportunity to meet a long term mystic.
During a lecture he was presenting on a mystic's role in society,
he uttered the words "inner warrior," while looking directly at
me. I had never met him and wondered if he knew I was the
author of **Mystic Warrior**. His lecture was fascinating and I
couldn't wait for a chance to speak to him without distraction.

In accord with the universal Law of Attraction, my intense
desire precipitated our quickly meeting. Less than an hour later,
at the hotel lunch buffet, he was walking towards my table,
carrying a plate of food. I jumped up and invited him to join us,
and he accepted.

I asked him whether he knew I had written **Mystic Warrior**.
Calmly, he smiled and answered that he didn't. He explained that
when he lectures, "It's not me who's speaking, but rather, the
'Master Within.'" He was referring to the divine aspect at the
heart of every soul—the universal source that all mystics strive
to tap into.

Then I asked him the question that his lecture had triggered
in me. "Is it permissible, from a mystic perspective, to use your
spiritual power to intervene and thwart the 'evil intentions' of
someone who is 'abusing an innocent?'"

From a mystic perspective, this question is profound. In the
mystic's view of the world all is one. There is no good vs. evil.
The cause of "evil" is ignorance.

I was asking the speaker, "What is worse: using your power
to control someone or allowing that someone to control another?"

This dilemma is the mystic equivalent of a Hollywood blockbuster plot crisis. In the movie, **Superman**, for example, it's when Superman has to decide between saving the world or Lois Lane. Either way, someone is going to lose. Philosophers describe it as "the lesser of two evils."

First, he explained that I was **assuming** the act to be evil, and that was only my perception. Next, he remarked that my perception of the abuse could also be mistaken. He went on to state that there could be a number of reasons why inaction might be better than action for all parties involved. Karma may be involved. The dispute may go back lifetimes. There was no possible way I could take into consideration all the factors that were governing the parties' dynamics and behavior. The best course of action would be for me to send unconditional love to both of them.

I held my tongue and told him I understood all that. Then I added, "What if you knew the person's motivation was pure self-interest?"

"How would you know?" he countered.

"What if the first party communicated that to you?"

He nodded, but repeated his assertion that the safest course of action was to send unconditional love.

Then I asked, "What if the abuse affected a large number of people?"

He paused and looked at me. He recognized that this was a topic I had pondered at great length. Every answer he had offered, I had already considered and came back with another question. That's when he asked, "Who is directing you?"

He wasn't referring to some external source. No, he was referring to one of the most fundamental teachings of mysti-cism, a teaching that has been expressed by numerous, great religions.

I smiled and he recognized that I understood him. I started to laugh.

I sat back in my chair, awed by the elegance of such a simple question and the thoughts it had spawned. The kingdom of God lies within. The goal of the evolving soul is to align his will with the Will of God. If you want to know how to handle any situation, consult the Master Within.

Now, while it's true that there are plenty of psychopaths who claim God told them to do some despicable act, our intuition and conscience signals to us that we can be confident they're mistaken. It seems worthy to note, here, that a person's understanding of the Master Within will change over time, as the person's wisdom increases, and his or her ability to attune with the Source of all creation improves.

But as a fundamental guide to how one should act in every situation, there is no simpler and more elegant advice than to ask for direction from The Master Within.

7

Creativity and Inspiration

The secret of creativity is learning how to attune with the One source of all creation. Mystics create their own personal sanctum on a higher plane to receive inspiration.

Creativity for the mystic has special meaning. As was stated earlier, in the world of the mystic, all is one. This means that there is only one Creator. Your job as an artist, painter or writer is simply to attune with this One Source of all creation, listen earnestly, and then "report" on what you have heard. This is the essence of divine inspiration. It's similar to the advice I was given as a young businessman, when my boss and I were on our way to an important meeting. He turned to me and said, "Keep your mouth shut and listen good."

As an author, I am most familiar with the art of writing, as compared with any of the other arts. Many people are fearful that they don't know how to write or that they're not qualified. Since everyone is tapping into the same source, this fear is groundless. All you have to do is, "Keep your mouth shut and listen good." Everyone is capable of writing effectively, because, as it turns out, God is an excellent writer.

Anyone can write. The secret is simply attuning with this One Source of creation. Writers attempt to do this by following certain routines or rituals. Rituals are simply a series of acts that are meant to impress upon the conscious mind what is being transmitted on a higher plane. Holy Communion, blessing of the food, or blowing a ram's horn are all examples of rituals. They are meant to put you in the proper state of mind, so that your attunement with the Source follows.

In the world of the writer, the rituals may involve writing at a certain time of day, with a favorite typewriter or at a certain desk. Smart writers try to recreate the same feelings they experienced when they were successful in pouring out material. A mystic takes this one step further, and you can do this, too.

Mystics create a personal sanctum that facilitates attunement with the one Creator. Now you can create one on the physical plane–a favorite recliner or special room for meditation or spiritual studies–but the more important one is on a higher plane. This is where you will go to receive inspiration.

Before you begin, decide what purpose you'd like to achieve. Then, decide what you'd like your private sanctum to look like. Will it be a nature scene with a waterfall or a babbling brook, a cathedral with majestic spires and translucent stained glass windows, a beach scene with waves gently lapping against the shore, or perhaps a garden with beautiful flowers? It doesn't matter what you choose, so long as you recognize it is safe.

After you relax with a few deep breaths, visualize yourself entering your sanctum. Use your inner senses to "look about." Feel yourself sitting on your chair. Notice the sounds and smells of your private space. When you are fully present, ask your question. Then simply listen and make a note of any impressions or intuitions you receive.

Understand, that when you return to the physical world, you may have to do some work, be it research, study, questioning, etc. In fact, one of the key reasons people suffer from writer's block is that they run out of material or don't have the knowledge to describe the information that's been given to them *in their personal sanctum*.

It's a good idea to visit your personal sanctum on a daily basis. There are additional benefits to this, such as increased vitality and tranquility, increased ability to concentrate, greater control of emotions, enhanced intuition, and the removal of fear and anxiety.

The prime benefit, however, of ascending to your own personal sanctum is to receive inspiration by direct attunement with God, the font of all creativity.

8

Balance: A Mystic Ideal

Having the left and right hemispheres of the brain in synch is the ideal state to transcend the mind and attune with God.

Last week, a friend of mine gave me a best-selling business book that forecast the rise of the right brain thinker and the demise of the left-brain thinker. Scientists have identified the right brain as the emotional, empathic, artistic side, and the left-brain as the side of logic, intellect and language. The essence of the author's argument is that we are moving from the age of information, which was dominated by computer programmers, MBAs and accountants, into a new conceptual age, which will be dominated by artists, caregivers and designers.

To many people with an interest in personal and spiritual growth, this is old news. A variety of tapes and CDs have been on the market since the early 1980s that were designed to influence brain rhythms, promoting greater balance and coherence, so that you can, in the words of one marketer, "meditate more deeply than a Zen monk."

What is remarkable is that the underlying mystic prin-ciples are *now* being accepted and transmitted to the general business public!

Albert Einstein once said, "No problem can be solved from the same level of consciousness that created it."

While producing great technological advances, our reliance on left-brain thinking has not necessarily advanced our evolution as a species. From the mystic perspective, however, neither would switching to a world dominated by artists and caregivers.

Once again, in the world of the mystic, all is one. This truism provides the answer as to which side of the brain we should use: BOTH!

The overriding goal should be BALANCE. Those who will thrive in the emerging spiritual age will be "whole-brainers." Using both sides of the brain in synchronization puts you in the proper state of mind, so that you can transcend mundane thinking and attune with God. You will think more clearly and improve your coordination, as well as derive the benefits described in our last chapter, such as increased vitality and tranquility, increased ability to concentrate, greater control of emotions, enhanced intuition, and the removal of fear and anxiety.

This is true no matter which side of your brain currently dominates. In the mystic's view, there is only one Creator. Your job as an artist is to attune with this One Source of all creation and report back your findings via your work, using both the creative skills and intuitions of your right hemisphere, and the logical, structural intelligence of your left hemisphere. Similarly, the engineer will never design anything of transcendent value by only relying on logic. An artist's sensibility and imagination must permeate the engineer's work, if the most highly prized designs and products are to be realized. In other words, you are selling yourself short by only relying on your one dominant hemisphere. For the greatest good, balance is vital.

The mystics most closely associated with the Jewish religion, the Kabalists, have a Tree of Life that illustrates the principle of balance. The Tree depicts in visual form ten interconnecting sephira, or aspects of God. Tifereth, the sephira of beauty, represents the ideal balance between justice and mercy. Lying in the center of the three columns, it is also the most direct path to the highest aspect of God.

The most direct method of attaining balance is through meditation. Meditators are taught to "center themselves," which synchronizes the brain hemispheres, as well as, brings about inner and outer balance. But meditation is *not* the only way. Any activity in which you feel pure joy, in which you lose yourself so completely that time passes without your conscious awareness, is one in which you are in balance. By definition, you have transcended time and space, which cannot be realized when you are locked into "single hemisphere" thinking. This can happen while you are walking, swimming, singing, dancing, playing a sport, communing with nature or making love.

A simple way to tell if you are "in synch" is by looking at a stereogram, which was popularized a few years back as pictures or posters consisting of a collection of black and white or colored dots. When the proper focus is attained, you are able to see a hidden picture within a picture. People who are overly dominant in either their left or right brain are unable to see the picture. When your brain is synchronized, you can see it. To view a text-based stereogram with a hidden word visit:

http://MysticWarrior.us/newsletter-image/

What's important is that in times of stress or fear, the brain will automatically return to its dominant side. Accountants will become more left brained and artists will become more right brained; neither of which is suitable if your goal is to attune with God and express your God-given gifts. Neither, alone, will help you evolve spiritually.

So the next time you're feeling frazzled and tense, pursue an activity that involves your whole mind and helps you connect with God. Turn off the TV and go for a walk, play with your children, or take 15 minutes to meditate. The influx of spirit into your being will not only reduce your anxiety, it will make the world a better place, as well.

9

Mystic Health

Observing these universal, dietary guidelines will not only improve your physical well-being, but also make it easier to attune with God, and aid in your spiritual development.

Quite often, when people hear the term "mystic," they immediately conjure up an image of someone with his or her head in the clouds, too busy contemplating spiritual concepts to be concerned with earthly matters. For a true mystic, nothing could be further from the truth.

Mystics are actually practical, pragmatic people. While a mystic's goal is direct communion with God, the primary purpose of this attunement is to bring this higher wisdom to earth and apply it. A healthy body is one key to making this possible.

Mystics regard the body as the "temple of the soul." Many ailments and illnesses have their basis in something that is non-physical, e.g., the mind. Psychologists sometimes refer to them as psychosomatic, and are the result of negative or mistake thoughts and beliefs. To help heal people who suffer from these maladies, mystics study, practice and master techniques such as psychic healing, energy healing or absent healing. While these spiritual practices can also heal many physical problems, to maximize their effectiveness, the physical causes of diseases should also be eliminated.

A body polluted with toxins or parasites is the primary cause of many illnesses. Filling your body with junk food and toxins depletes you of energy that you could put to better use, even if you are not sick. Just as you wouldn't try to run a race with a ball and chain tied to your ankle, neither should you allow your body to become a burden to your spiritual development.

Today, there are as many diets circulating with *conflicting* guidelines, as there are authors of diet books. Low-carb, low-fat, high protein, vegetarian, lactose-free, gluten-free are some of the more popular approaches. Based on your age, sex, level of fitness, weight, blood type, demeanor and your goals, any one diet might be better than another. From a mystic perspective, there are a few basics that are universally true.

Your body needs food, water and oxygen to operate effectively. The human body has evolved over thousands of years (perhaps millions). Common sense would tell you, it is unlikely that a chemist working in the lab of a multinational food corporation will design a food that is better for your body than Mother Nature. Time and time again, scientific evidence bears this out. You would do well to avoid manmade foods such as:

Artificial sweeteners: aspartame (Equal, NutraSweet), saccharin (Sweet & Low) and sucralose (Splenda). Over 75% of the complaints received by the FDA concern aspartame. A simple Google search for "adverse effects of aspartame" will shock you, and ensure that you never drink another diet soda in your life.

GMOs. Genetically Modified Organisms are foods that go beyond simple selective breeding to alter the genetic structure of the plant. Scientists, literally, force genes from one species into an entirely different species. The end result is the body does not know how to handle these foreign substances, which have only existed for the past 20 years. Studies have indicated genetically modified foods may contain pesticides, may trigger or exacerbate gluten-related disorders, can damage your intestinal wall and increase your risk of cancer and birth defects.

Fat-substitutes: Olean, Olestra and Benefat. If you read the labels of products containing these fat substitutes, you'll see such distressing potential side effects as "anal leakage." Don't try to trick your body by eating an indigestible fat in order to lose weight—the side effects are not worth it; plus, the long-term effects are unknown.

Hydrogenated and partially hydrogenated oils, also known as "fake fats" or "trans fats." These artificial fats are manufactured by adding hydrogen to vegetable oils and are found in margarine and processed foods. They can significantly increase your chances of heart disease and disrupt your metabolism. Many European countries ban or limit the amount of trans fatty acids in foods. Beginning January 1, 2006, US manufacturers are now required to list trans fats on the nutrition label, so that you can more readily avoid these "fake foods."

In his book, ***The Hidden Messages in Water***, Dr. Masaru Emoto demonstrated how thoughts and emotions affect the structure of water. Since our bodies are mostly water, it's clear your mental and emotional outlook will affect your health. Before you can even begin to worry about these effects, however, you need to make sure you have enough water in your body. Water is essential to flushing out toxins. Lack of water diminishes athletic, mental and spiritual performance. While moderate use of caffeine and alcohol is acceptable, remember that both will dehydrate your body, requiring you to drink even more water.

Most people do not get enough oxygen because they don't breathe properly. Shallow breathing, using only the top of your lungs, is not only inefficient; it allows a buildup of carbon dioxide, which is the primary waste product from the respiratory process. You should start each day with a few deep breaths that fully fill your lungs, followed by exhalations that completely empty them. If you have a respiratory ailment, this deep breathing may cause you to cough, which is exactly what you should be doing to eliminate the mucus surrounding the toxins in your lungs. When you are fatigued, deep breathing can invigorate you.

Caring for your body with these simple, common sense guidelines will not only help your physical wellbeing, but also make it easier to attune with God and aid in your spiritual development.

10

The Desire for Enlightenment

The desire for enlightenment arises out of a yearning from deep within the soul. It is not a physical, emotional or intellectual quest. Consequently, it's difficult to explain.

Yesterday, a marketing guru asked me a question that left me speechless.

I had retained Bob to review the copy on my **Mystic Warrior** website from a sales perspective. He asked about reader reactions. As we talked, I told him how some readers felt compelled, while in the midst of reading my book, to put it down and meditate. In several cases, they described tingling sensations on the crown of their head and of receiving "downloads of energy and information." I told Bob they were "attuning with God" and how this is a step towards enlighten-ment.

That's when he asked me the question that left me speech-less.

He asked, "Why would you want to be enlightened?"

Bob wasn't trying to be funny and he wasn't questioning whether this would benefit people. He asked me this to force me to think about the question in a more fundamental way. (You might say he was acting as a "devil's advocate.")

When I first heard his question, I couldn't respond. Going through my mind were the thoughts, "Isn't this what everybody wants?" and "Isn't this the reason for living?" But before I could even speak, I realized neither was true.

A belief is an idea that you accept as true—regardless of whether or not it really is. Many times a belief operates sub-consciously and is never examined, which is what had obviously happened with me. My belief in the two rhetorical questions above seemed self-evident, and yet, upon reflecting on Bob's question, this belief is likely *not* shared by most people. Not everyone wants to become enlightened—at least not consciously.

So I pondered some more: "Why *would* you want to be enlightened?"

This is not a simple question to answer. "Why would you want to be rich?" is easy to answer.

"So I can buy a new BMW M5."

"So I can travel throughout Europe staying at the finest hotels."

"So I can help others less fortunate than me."

The reason it's easy to answer is that being rich satisfies easily measurable, physical, emotional or intellectual desires.

Striving for enlightenment is not a physical, emotional or intellectual quest. It arises out of a yearning from deep within the soul to unite with your Divine Aspect or Higher Self. It's a craving to return to God, a desire to be completely and totally one with God.

Throughout the ages mystics have described this transcendent, sacred experience. Regardless of what formal religion the individual might practice (if any), the description of such experience almost always includes: a sense of being beyond time or space, yet connected to everything; boundless joy; unwavering knowingness; paradoxicality, yet unshakeable peace; ineffability. The experience might only last for seconds in earth time, yet leave the experiencer with permanent changes in his or her beliefs and outlook.

Anyone who has ever approached such an experience never forgets it. As Krishna said to Arjuna in *The Bhagavad Gita*: "A little of this knowledge dispels great darkness." After a taste of this bliss, nothing else compares. Consequently, you are no longer satisfied merely with great food, awesome sex, mind-blowing entertainment, or extravagant material goods. You want this glimpse of enlightenment to become permanent. You want to live in "Heaven on earth."

But the fact is, not everyone has this craving or is even aware it exists. So, short of sitting in the presence of an enlightened master, how do you awaken it in people? Does it trivialize the desire for enlightenment to say it will improve your life, that you'll lead a happier, less stressful life? Does it cheapen the quest for Self-realization to point out that as you move towards enlightenment and eliminate the veils (beliefs) that hide the true nature of God, that you'll begin to develop your inner senses, often referred to as psychic abilities?

Do you mention all of these benefits when someone asks, "Why would you want to be enlightened?"

Or do you simply smile and say, "Because nothing else matters."

11

7 Powerful Words of Wisdom

By allowing yourself to say "I changed my mind" and "I was wrong," you will experience newfound freedom. You will have taken 7 powerful steps towards the mystic virtue of wisdom.

"I changed my mind."

These are four of the most powerful words in the English language. They can prevent you from being manipulated into an undesirable outcome, and launch you forward on the road to personal and spiritual growth. Depriving yourself of the freedom to change your mind will lock you into a rigid mindset that can hamper your successes and your development.

Early in life, you may have been led to believe that it's not good to change your mind. There are numerous words with negative connotations associated with those who ***do*** change their minds: fickle, indecisive, hesitant, unsure, wavering, erratic or wishy-washy. You'd much prefer to be known as steadfast, decisive, confident and sure ... right?

Skilled manipulators use this near-universal conditioning against you every day. For example, has a salesman ever asked you, "Are you in a position to make a decision today?" Once you agree to this proposition, you'll feel pressure to "make a decision ***today***," and buy the product, even if you have reservations. After all, if you don't buy, you'd likely be considered "indecisive" by either the salesman or your own self-doubting ego.

But this is not what changing your mind is all about. Changing your mind means that after thinking about the subject or after gathering more complete information, you came to a different conclusion—a better and more ***informed*** decision. This is not being indecisive. It's being logical, prudent and wise.

Let's look at this matter from a different perspective. What would happen if you weren't **allowed** to change your mind? You'd spend all your free time watching cartoons, eating ice cream or playing tag. Or, more seriously, you'd be forced to believe the sun revolves around the earth. Your evolution on every level depends on your ability to assimilate new information and "change your mind" as to what it means and how it applies.

Psychologists call the unease you feel when you hold two conflicting opinions **cognitive dissonance**. The theory is that you will be naturally unwilling to simultaneously hold two apparently contradictory beliefs in your mind, and will attempt to modify one or the other to minimize the dissonance or conflict.

If you told the salesman that you "would be in a position to make a decision today," and yet, you actually felt that you needed more time to gather additional information and think it through, the uncomfortable feeling in your gut would mean that you were experiencing cognitive dissonance. The skilled salesman would then try to use this to push you into a buying decision **today**! If he lets you think it over, you may not make the purchase or may buy from someone else. For example, it's almost never a good idea to buy a new car after talking to only one dealer!

Imagine what would happen in instances involving somewhat more deep-seated beliefs. You think so-and-so is the best candidate, or such-and-such is the finest restaurant or this-or-that company produces the fastest car. To complicate matters, also imagine that you are on record as publicly stating that so-and-so is the best candidate, the finest restaurant is such-and-such or the fastest car comes from this-or-that company. You have invested your credibility in this belief. What happens when new evidence comes along that contradicts this deep-seated belief? Most likely, you'll immediately discount it.

Not only do you have the dissonance associated with trying to hold two contradictory beliefs in your mind simultaneously, but, even worse, if you accept the new idea, that might mean the first one was WRONG and you've lost your invested credibility!

How would most people handle the situation? Most people don't like being "wrong;" so, they would either ignore the new idea, or, even worse, come up with all sorts of counter arguments as to why it's wrong, vehemently defending their original position. In extreme cases, they may outright lie to others *and* to themselves, just to avoid the cognitive dissonance. To an independent observer, this appears totally irrational. To a student of human behavior, it is *understandable*.

As mystics, we're after the *truth*. Consequently, if it turns out that the second idea is more accurate, serves us better, or is otherwise superior to the first, we owe it to ourselves and to others to accept it, at least until a better idea comes along. We may be forced to utter three words that are even more powerful than "I changed my mind":

"I was wrong."

Being able to admit a mistake is a sign of humility, which is a prized mystic virtue. It does not mean you're a doormat or that you are subservient to somebody else. Acknowledging your having been mistaken about *anything*, and then changing your mind after gathering more complete information and thoroughly thinking things through is a sign of being logical, thorough, thoughtful and wise. Your prime allegiance is to the truth, regardless of where it originates.

There is tremendous freedom in uttering these powerful words. Your cognitive dissonance vanishes. You don't have to expend any energy defending the idea of "being right." You are free to pursue the truth without baggage.

Once you get into the habit of allowing yourself to say "I changed my mind" and "I was wrong" (7 words), you will experience newfound freedom. You will have taken 7 powerful steps towards the mystic virtue of wisdom.

12

Thought Manifestation

Avoid manifesting a NEGATIVE outcome from a POSITIVE situation by following this simple principle.

The universe just conspired to remind me of a valuable lesson.

Last night, before retiring, I was trying to think of a marketing promotion for **Mystic Warrior**, something that would properly express and emphasize the overwhelmingly positive response I've received from readers. You see, out of thousands of readers, not a single person had taken me up on my unconditional money-back guarantee.

The image that came to me was that of the old TV commercial showing a lonely Maytag repairman, whose products were so reliable that no one ever had a problem. Every time the phone rang, the repairman would grab it, hoping that it would be a complaint.

I thought to myself, "What if I write about a fictitious reader who returned a book, drawing attention to this exception?"

I dismissed the idea as untruthful. Fortunately, I had no "unhappy readers."

Meetings occupied me the next morning. After returning to my office after lunch, I discovered an unhappy reader had emailed me!

My fleeting thought had manifested in less than 12 hours.

The mystic or spiritual principle that was demonstrated to me is a basic one. It comes in several flavors:

"Whatever you think about expands."

"You are what you think."

"Be careful what you wish for—you just might get it."

These are all applications of the Law of Attraction, or Like attracts Like. Everything is energy; everything has its own unique frequency. You automatically attract energies of a similar frequency. The energy of a thought will attract similar energies to it. Reflecting on my experience, I realized that I was well acquainted with these principles, which form the basis of many mystic visualization exercises (for example, as were described in *3 Steps to Manifesting Your Ideal Life*).

What surprised me, though, was not that my thought actually manifested, or that it did so as quickly as it did. Thoughts can sometimes manifest instantly! Neither was it that so little time had been spent thinking this particular thought. What *was* shocking was that I had manifested a NEGATIVE outcome, by reflecting on a very POSITIVE situation!

That was my lesson.

Even though my conscious mind was hearing positive thoughts, such as "There has not been a single unhappy reader," it's a different story for the subconscious mind. The subconscious mind doesn't know the difference between positive or negative thoughts.

The words "no, never, not" have no meaning for the subconscious mind! For example, if I were to order you, "Do NOT think of a pink elephant in the middle of the room," what do you think your subconscious mind would focus on?

Similarly, what my subconscious mind heard was: "... blah blah blah, *unhappy reader*." It didn't matter that there weren't any; all it heard was the focus of my thought. Then in less than 12 hours, an unhappy reader manifested to demonstrate the principle to me.

It was as if a huge, delicious donut was staring me in the face, which was so big it didn't have a hole. But instead of looking at the plump donut, I was thinking, "This donut has NO hole." The universe heard me and quickly manifested a hole.

You may have heard the old adage, "Don't focus on what you *don't* want; focus on what you *do* want." This is a good way of ensuring that you stay positive and avoid the negative. But for a mystic, there is more that can be done. You can phrase your desire so that there are only *positive* elements in it. This way, your subconscious mind will not misinterpret what you're saying.

For example, let's say you suffer from headaches. You might be content to be "pain-free." Desiring this outcome will probably help very little, if at all. It'd be better to strive to be "healthy and clear-headed."

In other words, you should choose to:

Be healthy, not pain-free.
Be pro-peace, not anti-war.
Be clean and sober, not anti-drug.
Be pro-environment, not anti-pollution.
Be wealthy, not debt-free.

When you incorporate this principle into your thoughts and words, and state them clearly, the universe will conspire to make them come true!

13

Synchronicities

Synchronicities, or meaningful coincidences, occur frequently when you are "in the flow." Learning to recognize and appreciate synchronicities will aid you in living a life of ease and grace.

Almost everyone has had experiences where they think of something, and coincidentally it appears: a person you hadn't seen in years shows up unexpectedly; a trial issue of a magazine is delivered to your home with just the information you needed; or you flip on the car radio to hear the lyrics of a song, which provides you with the answer to a burning question you'd had.

These meaningful coincidences, or synchronicities, are examples of the universe conspiring to provide you with what you need or most truly want. If your goal is to live a life of ease and grace, it would behoove you to learn to recognize and appreciate these synchronicities, for these are times when you are undoubtedly "in the flow."

Some scientists do not believe in synchronicities. They look at the universe as a mechanical, deterministic system, without taking into consideration the role of consciousness. They label these instances as mere coincidences, and find statistical measures to explain them away. There is even a term known as "observer bias" that says when you are looking for a specific item or event, you are much more likely to notice it. An example would be if you wanted to buy a red Ford Taurus, then you'd likely begin to notice them everywhere.

It's true that you are more likely to notice an object that you desire; but from a mystic perspective, observer bias is, at best, an incomplete explanation. As mystics, we are 100% supportive of science and logical thinking. But by incorporating the role of consciousness into our paradigm (world view), we have a better and more accurate predictor of events. This is good science.

By thinking about a specific item, you are invoking the Law of Attraction. As was explained in our last chapter, *Thought Manifestation*, everything is energy. Everything has its own unique frequency and you automatically attract energies of a similar frequency. The energy of a thought will attract similar energies to it.

If your thoughts are filled with red Ford Tauruses, then you'll attract them to you. If your objective is to **own** a red Taurus, then begin visualizing yourself **driving** the car, not just **seeing** it on the road or on TV, just as was explained in *3 Steps to Manifesting Your Ideal Life*.

The Law of Attraction is the underlying basis for these synchronicities.

Scientists estimate the processing capacity of the conscious mind at 2,000 bits of information per second, compared to 4 billion bits per second for the subconscious mind. Clearly, the subconscious mind is far more powerful. Your external world is a reflection of your thoughts, feelings and beliefs. Since the vast majority of the thoughts you are sending out to the universe are beyond the awareness of your conscious mind, it's your **internal** thoughts, feelings and beliefs that are most influential.

When your thoughts are jumbled, you're sending out inconsistent signals. The world will likely appear as a chaotic, unpredictable place, since your conscious mind's desires are contradicted by your internal thoughts, feelings and beliefs.

When your conscious mind is congruent with your internal world, you are sending out consistent signals. The universe responds and you recognize how everything just comes together. As this state of "coherent consciousness" becomes more deeply established, your life will be filled with more synchronicities, as your external world more accurately reflects your inner thoughts. When sports stars are "in the flow," they often describe the game as slowing down and becoming effortless. Naturally, you are also more likely to recognize a coincidence (observer bias); but by having your internal and external worlds congruent, you are not just aware of it, but influencing its manifestation.

How can you develop this state of coherent consciousness? Know thyself.

It's your responsibility and privilege to create incidents that you truly want by being more mindful of your thoughts. Recognize whenever you are "in the flow," and take note of your thoughts and what you are doing. At the least, this is what you were meant to be doing at that particular moment in time. If you see a pattern, recognize that these thoughts and actions may be your life's work.

Remember, at your very core lies the Master Within, or your divine self. Your goal as a mystic is to attune with the Master Within, as you seek to become one with God. When you do this, your conscious mind and internal thoughts, feelings and beliefs will become congruent, and synchronicities will become a way of life.

When all of these aspects of your being are radiating energy "in synch," miracles may occur. But it's not a miracle—it's a direct result of a perfectly understandable universal law. A bumper sticker states, "We don't *believe* in miracles, we *rely* on them." Similarly, don't believe your life is a random series of coincidences—***make it miraculous***.

14

Reincarnation

Your past lives represent another component of what makes you tick. An understanding of reincarnation is a tool that can add a depth of understanding to certain situations, especially relationships.

Last week, a reader wrote to say, "Why would I want to waste time wondering if I lived as an Incan, or as anyone else? I have enough to do in this lifetime!"

The reader was referring to a comment I'd sent out in an email regarding an upcoming spiritual journey to Machu Picchu and Peru. While the tone of my "Incan comment" was meant to be light-hearted, the reader had a point. The purpose of looking at past lives is not meant to distract you from your responsibilities in your current life. Nor is it to provide you with another area of study that must be mastered in order to "graduate."

You can live a perfectly happy life, filled with personal and spiritual growth, without any reflection on the subject of reincarnation. In fact, one mystic sect, Sufism, discourages it, since they believe study of reincarnation diverts its disciples from the ultimate goal of attaining Oneness with God.

So why *does* anyone care about reincarnation?

Virtually all religions point to the existence of a soul—the aspect of you that is not physical—and agree that this soul is everlasting. Reincarnationists hold the view that this everlasting soul incarnates many times in order to provide the depth and breadth of life experiences that allow for one's spiritual evolution to higher consciousness or higher dimensions. This is a logically consistent explanation for the trials and tribulations we face on earth.

To reject the idea of reincarnation is to introduce a randomness to the universe that is inconsistent with the idea of a benevolent, compassionate and fair God. For example, why should one child be born to a loving family with all physical, emotional and spiritual needs being met, while another is born to a drug-addicted mother with no home nor means of support? What could possibly be fair about such an imbalance of fortune, unless the idea is taken into consideration that this is but one of that soul's many incarnations.

While it is no measure of the validity of a theory, the majority of the population on earth today believes in reincarnation. It was a common belief in the time of Jesus, and nothing that Jesus was alleged to have said was inconsistent with this belief. Father Origen, one of the top theologians of the church around 200 AD, wrote frequently on the subject. It was not until 545 AD that the Fifth Ecumenical Council declared the concept of reincarnation heretical, obviously for political reasons.

So why care about *your* particular past lives?

Your past lives represent another component of what makes you tick—who you are now—how you got where you are—and who you might become later, either in this incarnation or the next. In his book, ***Many Lives, Many Masters***, Dr. Brian Weiss was surprised to discover some of his patients would recall past life traumas that proved to the basis for their current problems. By addressing these traumas, even though they had occurred in past lives, he was able to help heal his patients.

My study of mysticism was triggered years ago by a vivid past life recall while watching a Dick Sutphen video. Prior to that moment, my interest in spiritual subjects and history was minimal; but after investigating the information that was revealed during my spontaneous recall, my perspective changed. My recall of that life was entirely consistent with that time period, and there was no other explanation for how I could have learned of it. Clearly, my formal education had been incomplete.

Now, I recognize that an understanding of reincarnation is a tool that can add a depth of understanding to certain situations, especially relationships. On several occasions in this lifetime, I have interacted with others in ways that would appear strange to an independent observer, but become perfectly understandable when acts from prior lifetimes are considered.

In one instance, within an hour of meeting me, a woman asked me to follow her to her home, where she inexplicably handed me two ceramic eagles and told me they were for me. I later discovered it was her way of apologizing for taking my sons away from me hundreds of years earlier. On another occasion, I was at a loss to understand why I continued to help a talented, but self-sabotaging drunk. Upon later reflection, I recognized him as having saved my life in a previous lifetime. Unconsciously, I felt obligated to return the favor, and he provided plenty of opportunities for me to do so. In both cases, these actions would have happened with or without my conscious knowledge of a prior connection; but I derived additional satisfaction from the knowledge that our interactions were complete, and we had found our way to a proper closure.

Not everything is related to past lives, and not every act requires such introspection. But if you find yourself experiencing a sense of déjà vu, or wondering why you feel compelled to act outside of your normal character, you may want to reflect on it in the light of reincarnation and past lives. There is the chance that a past life is involved, and you may derive some valuable insights from its contemplation.

I'm looking forward to taking a trip with a group interested in mysticism this year, a *Sacred Journey to Peru* and hope that I get to experience that sense of déjà vu. The Incas had connections with the ancient continent of Lemuria (Mu), and the Pleiades constellation (the Seven Sisters of Greek Mythology). The only way to access these connections is in the eternal NOW, which I hope to do in Peru.

15

Predicting the Future

The best way to predict the future is to create it.

Last week, a friend of mine forwarded me an invitation to an upcoming remote viewing conference in England. Remote viewing is the ability to "see," without using your normal physical senses, objects or events that are remotely located from you in either time or space. In the invitation, the instructor described how Associative Remote Viewing (ARV) could be used to predict the future. The example he gave was this: suppose you wanted to know who would win a football game being played the next day. Rather than ask a remote viewer, "Who will win the game?", it'd be wiser to associate an apple, for example, with the first team winning and a pencil with the second team winning. You would then ask the remote viewer, "Please describe the object that I will hand to you tomorrow," (hence, "Associative" Remote Viewing).

Later that day, my friend asked me to elaborate.

I told him there are two aspects to this process.

First, you can use your intention to create any association you want. Advertisers create associations by playing a certain song or music while they pitch you to buy their product. Whenever you hear that song play you associate their product with it. Similarly, you can associate a positive mental state with a word or hand gesture, such as pulling your ear lobe. After you do this often enough, you can then use the word or hand gesture to induce the positive mental state you desire.

In a more profound example of using associations, suppose you wanted to help someone using prayer or energy healing. It doesn't matter where that person is located; all you have to do is associate an image of the person needing help with the person, by visualizing them standing in front of you. Flood your image of them with love and energy. Since quantum physics has demonstrated that time and space can be transcended by intention, he or she will get the benefit, regardless of their distance from you. It is more convenient to simply visualize an image of the person needing help, and then take action, than it would be to travel across the world to address them in person. You, as the healer, are operating in the field of consciousness, beyond time and space; so it doesn't matter WHEN, either, although it's always better to visualize NOW, i.e., the eternal present.

Second, from a mystic perspective, we are all connected; there is only the "One" thing. All of our perceptions are tiny aspects of this One thing. That is why, when we are on top of our game, everything appears as a synchronicity; as everything *has* to be related, since there is only the One thing. The difficulty arises from our inability to see the One thing, due to our limited perspective. On the physical plane, our perspective is further limited by the restrictions of time and space. Operating in the 3D world, we cannot see all possible futures, which exist simultaneously.

The future we eventually experience is the one that our collective beliefs and desires attract. Individually, we could attract a new mate or a new job, for instance; yet this individual attraction operates in conjunction with what the group or society, as a whole, chooses to attract. What we attract is not etched in stone—obviously, people can change their minds or beliefs. From our 3D perspective, the future is therefore not fixed; but some scenarios are more likely than others, based on the Law of Attraction.

What does this have to do with predicting the outcome of a football game?

In ALL types of remote viewing, the remote viewer is able to get a perspective that is outside of the limiting 3D perspective, again, beyond time and space. Remote viewers are not omniscient, as they are still not capable of viewing the One thing in its entirety. What the remote viewer would most likely perceive is the event/scenario that has the most energy associated with it.

Associative Remote Viewing was developed specifically to keep the conscious mind, with all its biases and preconceptions, out of the equation. By associating a previously unrelated object to an event or target, versus just asking or even providing actual physical coordinates, there is less chance the remote viewer's conscious mind will interfere and jump to conclusions. It's not the Associative aspect that allows peering into the future—all remote viewing can do this. ARV is simply better at keeping the mind at bay.

In the experiment designed to choose one of two outcomes to a football game, by associating different objects with each outcome, the remote viewer's biases and desires would be minimized. Theoretically, he or she would choose the object with the most energy and consequently, the outcome with the higher likelihood of occurring. This system is not infallible, as remote viewers are capable of human error; the interpretation of the remote viewer's findings may not be accurate; and, as mentioned earlier, the energy may shift so that what was previously identified as the more likely event may no longer occur.

How can you use this knowledge to predict the future?

Recognize that the future is not fixed. All possible futures exist simultaneously and the one that we experience is the one with the greatest collective energy associated with it. Visualize the scenario that you desire and ignore any negative or limiting opinions of others. Any individual or institution that tells you differently is either ignorant or deliberately attempting to limit your future options. As you practice, you will increase your effectiveness. You will attract others of like mind, and influence those who surround you, who will help your desires to manifest.

The best way to predict the future is to create it.

16

The Near Death Experience and Truth

*The NDE offers an alternative perspective on
Truth that can add to your understanding of life.*

Recently, I attended a meeting of the Fort Lauderdale
Chapter of the International Association for Near Death Studies.
IANDS' stated mission is to provide reliable information about
near-death experiences (NDEs) to experiencers, caregivers,
researchers and the public. It also serves as a community for
people to discuss their life-changing experiences.

I was fascinated to hear some of these experiences directly
from the people who lived through them. The people who chose
to speak were everyday people, with regular jobs, leading
traditional lives. They were not researchers and they had no
biases or theories to defend. Each person simply described what
had happened to him or her. What distinguished many of the
experiencers from the general public were that those who had
undergone a NDE were filled with compassion for others; some
of them were radiating love with such intensity that it was
palpable.

One experiencer's story captured many of the themes that
were often repeated by the others in the group: After being
pronounced dead, the man described meeting his deceased father
in an out-of-body experience. He flew in a beautiful environment
towards a fantastic sunset, while basking in a sea of love. He
emphasized how nothing on earth ever compared to the feelings
of love he experienced, and how it was impossible to explain it.
"You would have to be there to understand," he said.

Listening to their accounts, I was also struck by the
similarity between the near death experience and the mystical
experience. Both are transcendent, timeless experiences that
confirm we are, indeed, "spiritual beings having a human

47

experience." The major difference is that no one is pronounced dead in a mystical experience.

Both share a sense of the out-of-body experience (OBE), the intense feelings of love/bliss, the timelessness, the inability to describe the experience with words, and a knowingness that transcends rational thought. In this state, you can hold two contradictory thoughts in your head simultaneously and recognize that both are true.

From the mystic perspective, consciousness is a continuum from our separate, mundane physical life to the unity experience where everything is connected and experienced as nothing other than ourselves. Out-of-body experiences, remote viewing, telepathy, and precognitive glimpses into the future are all intermediate steps towards the ultimate union with the All-That-Is.

Our group discussed their experiences with some of these phenomena, similarities to the NDE, and how they can help in our spiritual development.

One of the attendees (not an experiencer) stated, "You shouldn't seek out-of-body experiences. Our mission is to stay put on earth."

Several of the experiencers disagreed strongly. "You can go wherever you like," they argued. "The physical world isn't real, anyway."

The woman who criticized OBEs responded, "We incarnate on earth to learn important life lessons until we are advanced enough to graduate to a higher world. This is com-monly accepted wisdom."

The experiencers wouldn't accept this. None of them claimed to have any formal metaphysical training upon which to base his or her opinion. But, each had a unique near death experience that seemed to contradict the woman's logic. One of them summed it up, "There are no rules. All that matters is love."

The group was at an impasse. Which was correct?

From a mystic viewpoint, both were. Very often, all that matters is the perspective you use to view an issue. Seen from our 3D physical perspective, complete with time and space, it appears we reincarnate, learn lessons and advance spiritually. But seen from a perspective in which time and space do not exist, these rules appear arbitrary and limiting. As the experiencers agreed, "All that exists is love."

I suggested that incarnation on earth is an opportunity to do exactly as the woman suggested. But, it's *an opportunity, not an obligation*. This seemed to satisfy most people.

There are very few ideas that are universally true. Even the mystic concept of reincarnation only makes sense in a world with time and space. Your viewpoint is critical in determining the "truth." So, from whatever perspective you choose to view the world, be sure that it aligns with your own highest truth. And, just like the experiencers, continue to operate from a viewpoint of compassion and love. The truth will be a lot more pleasurable when you do.

17

Spiritual Arrogance

Even spiritually gifted individuals can be slowed down by "spiritual arrogance." Here's how to avoid the pitfalls.

Last week, I received an email from a reader stating, "I have evolved past the spiritual understanding of author."

I chuckled at the reader's bluntness. He didn't mince words; clearly, he felt that he had developed capabilities that were not only greater than those of "author," but beyond the "understanding of author."

Whether or not this is true is beside the point. No doubt there are readers with abilities that are greater than mine, and these may be beyond my understanding. The issue is not your level of development, but the fact that you are striving to develop. One of the keys to growth is recognizing that there is always room for improvement.

In any field, whether it's sports, the arts, your profession, or spiritual growth, there are always going to be some people who are further along in their development than others. We live in a society where "trash-talking" basketball stars and egomaniacal real estate moguls are idolized. Inevitably, there will be people who feel the need to tell you how much better they are than you. In the area of spiritual development, this is known as "spiritual arrogance."

By its nature, spiritual arrogance is exclusionary. Unlike the mystic understanding that All is One, people suffering from spiritual arrogance will tell you "they are advanced," implying that "you are not." Some of the worst offenders are those who have some understanding of the spiritual laws that govern the universe, who have opened some of their inner senses, and who say they are on the path to enlightenment. Where they go astray is when they pronounce themselves "gurus."

When that happens, a difference of opinion is often assumed to be an attack on their mastery. I once heard a gifted woman dismiss someone who disagreed with her by explaining, "He's not one of the 144,000," implying that he was not one of the chosen ones in the Book of Revelation, but that she was. Clearly, humility is not one of her virtues.

At other times, people have recommended that I sign up for workshops by self-proclaimed avatars, whose God-ordained mission is to single-handedly save the earth. Naturally, I appreciate the encouragement that I continually expand my consciousness. However, I believe we were given the powers of discernment and a discriminating intellect to separate the wheat from the chaff.

Last year, at a metaphysical conference, an entertainer captured the essence of this illusion in song. He sang a parody of Carly Simon's classic, *You're so Vain*, renamed *You're so Light*. Lyrics included, "All your friends thought that you were enlightened, you were enlightened. You're so light. You probably think you don't have a shadow. Don't you? Don't you?" The audience was rolling with laughter, because they all knew someone who fit that description.

There are two major drawbacks to this behavior:

1) It inhibits your own development. When you believe that you "know everything," there's no room for additional wisdom. This should be self-evident; but additionally, just giving the impression of "knowing everything" can deter people from sharing their knowledge with you. Who wants to be told, "I already know that!"? This attitude of spiritual arrogance effectively shuts off sources of new knowledge. Remember, a wise man can learn more from a fool than a fool from a wise man; and God speaks through everyone, not just avatars.

2) It wastes energy. Anyone who has staked out a position as a guru is forced to conform to this new self-image. This places

an unnecessary burden on them. Why burden yourself with having to live up to the expectations of some image? Why waste energy trying to uphold such an image? Why not *be* exactly who you are, so as to let your true inner self shine through without filters?

In contrast to spiritual arrogance, a trait common to long-term mystics is their humility. Unlike the basketball world, there is no trash talking. Attuning with God is not a competitive sport. There is no need to live up to exaggerated claims or false images.

Most long-term mystics recognize that they are a part of the One. Seeing themselves as both teachers and students, they help those who might not be as far along in their studies in one area, and are open to learn from others who are more proficient than they in another area (just as more advanced mystics have helped *and* learned from them in their earlier days). With this viewpoint, they recognize that the spiritually arrogant are merely passing through a phase, much as was described in *The Surrender of the Ego*.

True humility involves the willingness and open-mindedness to accept help and insight from all sources. In **Mystic Warrior**, the hero, Alec Thorn, illustrates this trait by his willingness to accept guidance from an unlikely source—a seemingly meek and mild-mannered florist. Sophie turns out to be one of the wisest, most powerful characters in the book. Conversely, other characters, oozing with spiritual arrogance, reject outside advice and focus solely on "humbling" Thorn. The interaction between the heroes and the villains in this spiritual thriller not only illustrates the mythological dynamic between "good and evil," but also demonstrate valuable lessons about walking the path of a mystic in life.

Much needless pain can be avoided by recognizing the symptoms of spiritual arrogance. Don't worry that you might not recognize a true avatar, if one ever does cross your path. There's a foolproof method for identifying them: "You will know them by their fruits."

18

Your Influence Counts

By choosing to ignore certain aspects of your life, you are delegating your experience to others who have a greater interest in the outcome. Their interest may not be your interest.

Many people are so alienated with the political process in the United States that they will not bother to vote in next week's midterm elections. They feel our political system is so corrupt, it doesn't matter who's in power—that politicians only act to get reelected and maintain their perks of office. To some, voting is just like putting a fresh coat of paint on a condemned building.

These beliefs are self-defeating. They make people feel powerless and turn people away, not only from the political process, but also from life. To those who would profit from the current state of affairs, this is exactly what they would have you do. To effect change, you must remain connected: *your influence counts!*

As was outlined earlier in *3 Steps to Manifesting Your Ideal Life*, one of the key factors in manifestation is to identify what it is you want. Our consensus reality is a weighted average of everyone's beliefs. When you choose to ignore certain aspects of your life, you are "not voting," you are delegating your experience to others who have a greater interest in the outcome. Remember, though: their interest may *not* be your interest.

In the political arena, there are far more honest citizens of good will than there are corrupt politicians. In the long run, the virtuous will win. This must be kept in mind at all times. Despair is the weapon of those who would seek to maintain the corrupt system.

As many people sense, a new world is emerging. Every day more and more service workers are awakening. Those seeking to maintain the corrupt system will attempt to convince you "resistance is futile." Understand that these are the last gasps of the negative forces who see their power waning.

You rarely see reports of the virtuous overcoming the corrupt on the news—much more frequent are the horror stories of self-dealing and corruption. This is also important, as Carl Jung once explained, "One does not become enlightened by imagining figures of light, but by making the darkness conscious." The corruption must be exposed, and a vision of truth and honesty must replace it. This is everyone's job.

At the highest levels of world government on our planet, above the visible figures you see on television, there are political forces in conflict. This has nothing to do with the "Republican versus Democrat" paradigm. Behind the scenes, many positively oriented elites are helping humanity. By envisioning a positive world, you will help it to come about.

Dramatic changes are happening; they're just not yet visible in the physical world. An analogy is monitoring the temperature of a glass of ice water placed in a warm room. Even though the ice is melting, the temperature will remain fixed at 32 degrees F. Only when the ice is gone will the temperature start to rise.

You can speed up the manifestation of the world you'd like to see by constantly reminding yourself that you influence events based on your beliefs and your actions. Know, also, that these effects manifest over time; instant results are rare.

In these transitional times, do not become discouraged. Help is always available by tapping into the Master Within. Remember that everything is as it should be. It's virtually impossible to make sense of all the little details to see the bigger picture. That would require vastly expanded consciousness, which very few have on earth.

Do not be concerned solely with the immediate, outward manifestation of your efforts. Pay attention to inner urges to take action. There is divine timing in everything, especially when one is heeding the voice of the Master Within.

Breakthroughs in your individual growth are timed to coincide with the spiritual breakthroughs of others for a greater good. It's not a linear world, where everyone's efforts manifest independently. The return to the One involves everyone, including those who are slower to awaken. Greater societal transformation occurs when an entire wave of individuals awaken together. In this light, the exposure of any existing corruption can be viewed as a stimulus to the awakening process.

To those of you who are waiting for your brothers and sisters to wake up, remain patient. Keep in mind, if you are too far in front of the curve, no one knows what you're doing and your efforts will not yet be appreciated. You are developing your spiritual muscles. In time, your efforts will bear fruit.

So go ahead and vote for the candidate who best matches the vision you have for our world. The effect may seem subtle, but it is real, nonetheless. Your influence counts!

19

Reality and Innovation

Don't let "reality" get in your way the next time you're asked to come up with an innovative solution to some problem. Chances are it's only a limiting belief that's holding you back.

This past week, a reader forwarded me an article from **Business Week**, entitled *Is Reality the Enemy of Innovation?* The author explained that what we think of as "reality" is merely a model, which can change. He cited examples of scientific theories that had changed over time, and **concluded** that if we keep this in mind, we have a better chance of **creating the future** vs. **reinforcing the past**.

This is excellent advice. Knowing that these models can change is liberating, especially when contrasted with the view of reality as fixed. While very helpful, however, from the mystic viewpoint, the article only scratches the surface.

The reality that you perceive is not merely a model that is subject to change. Reality is almost entirely a function of your beliefs, which are ideas you accept as true, but are not necessarily so. Everything you see, hear, smell, taste and feel is filtered and interpreted via your underlying beliefs. Your entire life experience is a function of your beliefs. Consequently, your beliefs are one of the most important components of your future success.

If you are seeking to innovate or striving for a goal, whether it's designing a new product, attracting a mate, getting fit or creating abundance, your beliefs will profoundly influence your likelihood of success.

Henry Ford explained this concisely: "Whether you think you can or think you can't—you are right."

If you are not attaining your goals, the problem most likely is not that you lack the knowledge to accomplish them, but rather that you have preconceived ideas, i.e., beliefs that act as obstacles to your success.

Often it's more important to UNLEARN than it is to LEARN.

A friend of mine wanted to take up fly fishing, which involves casting to a particular spot in a mountain stream, an act that would seem to require great skill. Ray didn't know anything about this sport, and so he called Greg, a tournament fly caster, to ask how long it would take for Greg to teach him to become proficient at casting.

Greg asked, "Do you have any prior experience?"

Ray said, "No."

Greg said, "I can teach you to become an exceptional fly caster in less than an hour."

"How is that possible?" Ray asked, more than a little incredulous. "My neighbors have been fishing for *years* and they still haven't got it down."

Greg explained, "That's exactly the problem. Teaching them would take a lot longer, because I have to get them to unlearn everything that they've previously been taught."

In other words, it's not what you ***don't*** know that can stop you; it's what you ***think*** you know—which may or may not be true.

Experienced venture capitalists and business financiers often joke that many entrepreneurs would never start new companies if they knew how the odds were stacked against them and all the unseen obstacles that lay in their path.

Typically, these entrepreneurial risk takers don't have advanced degrees, and that's the point. They just act without preconceived notions. The entrepreneurs don't know about and don't focus on potential limitations. Thank heaven they don't— the world would be devoid of much innovation if "reality" intruded on their visionary minds.

Here's a mystic "trick" that often helps with beliefs:

If you're like most people, you probably identify beliefs as either true or false. A more constructive way would be to characterize them as "supportive" or "non-supportive" to your stated goal. By doing this, you defuse any emotions you might have with them, and unlink your beliefs from previous associations that may lock you into preconceived attitudes or behaviors. So, don't worry if your beliefs are true or false. Just pay attention to whether they clearly support your intentions or not.

A wise objective, in other words, would be to UNLEARN, ELIMINATE, or NEUTRALIZE non-supportive beliefs and *only* accept supportive beliefs, regardless of whether you might think of them as true or false.

Remember, you can always find some evidence to support one belief over another. Furthermore, based on the electrical patterns that fire in your brain, your brain can't tell the difference between an actual experience or one that you're imagining. You may as well choose beliefs that are supportive.

So don't let "reality" get in your way the next time you're asked to come up with an innovative solution to some problem, or would like to attain some goal that you've set for yourself. Chances are it's only a limiting belief that's holding you back. Act in spite of your fears. Just do it and chances are, you'll surprise yourself.

All that can stop you is you.

20

Travel to Enlightenment

*Travel is one of the fastest and most effective
ways to gain insight into yourself and the world—an
accelerated learning environment for personal
growth and development.*

Traveling through Hong Kong, Beijing, Taiwan and Tibet,
I am reminded of, not only, how enjoyable it is to directly
experience new people, places, cultures and beliefs, but also how
stimulating travel is to our personal growth and development.
Travel is one of the fastest and most effective ways to gain insight
into yourself and the world. Rusty Schweikhart, an astronaut who
flew on both Apollo 9 and 11, captured this sentiment when he
said: "Outer and inner exploration go hand-in-hand."

As was stated earlier, the Law of the Triangle states that
when two opposites come together, there is the potential to create
a third entity. By encountering new and different stimuli, you are
prodded into examining your previous beliefs. Conversely, when
there is no new stimulus, there is no incentive to change—you
tend to stagnate.

By traveling, you can consciously act to discover
differences that have the potential to create new perspectives for
you, as well as seed new ideas in others. Travel can be an
accelerated learning course, in which you are motivated to
expand and modify your previous assumptions about life.

Most great spiritual teachers have spent at least some time
traveling. While obviously the teacher desires to share his or her
knowledge, which is made easier by traveling, there is also the
direct, stimulating effect of travel itself.

Buddha's life story of forsaking the cloistered walls of his
father's kingdom to explore the world is a case in point. He was
unaware of the poverty and lack of wisdom that prevailed in his

father's kingdom. Only by travel did this knowledge reach him and inspire his quest for enlightenment, which he later shared to influence billions of people.

Moses, Jesus, Mohamed and John the Baptist all spent time in the desert or on a mountaintop. While the mountaintop is a metaphor for communing with God, in the more literal sense, both actions represent a change in the immediate environment as a means to gain expanded consciousness and insight. In these cases, it is a lack of external stimulation that is sought, which eases access to your inner senses.

If you are like most people, you spend a vast amount of time reliving your past or, conversely, worrying about your future. While is it is possible to affect your experience of the past by using such mystic techniques as Mental Alchemy, the most powerful place to be is "the present." After all, only by acting in the present can you affect your future.

Travel is a built-in mechanism to induce you to stay in the present by focusing your attention on the newness of the "here and now."

We are all creatures of habit. A man who shaves will begin his shaving ritual by starting on one side of his face and will invariably continue to do so for the next 60 years of his life. Most people will drive along the same path to the office on a daily basis. Given this routine way of living, it's easy to pass an exciting or noteworthy event and ignore it, as you have placed yourself into a virtual trance.

Any time your mind "knows" or you say, "I know that," there is a tendency to shut off any potential for learning. This is not the ideal environment for insights to arise.

Travel stimulates your mind by exposing you to new activities. There are so many new ideas and objects to explore in a new or foreign place, that your mind does not have the chance to say, "I know that." By traveling, you are naturally living life out of your normal routine, spontaneously engaging more in the present moment, and creating a highly effective environment in which to grow and develop your consciousness.

Whether traveling or not, synchronicities occur far more readily when you are living in the present. This is partly because you recognize these meaningful coincidences when they occur; but more importantly, it is because you are able to tap into your subconscious mind. When you are in the present, you are in the flow of life and you are acting to manifest these coincidences. Certainly, I seem to find that synchronicities occur more often when I'm traveling, and that adds even more richness and happiness to my journeys.

One of the greatest gifts I have ever received came while traveling. I was waiting to meet with my friends Mark and Andrea to plan for last year's *Sacred Journey to Peru*. Eating a continental breakfast at the Inn of Sedona, my eyes locked onto a beautiful Chinese woman who entered the room radiating joy. I waited for her to approach my table and asked her to join me. She considered it, but declined my invitation, preferring to sit at a counter overlooking the beautiful red mountains of Sedona.

I thought about joining her immediately, but dismissed the idea as being too forward. I waited for another opportunity to ask her to join me, which came a few minutes later when she arose to get some fruit. This time, she accepted my invitation and we discussed our many shared interests in travel, spirituality and healing. When she learned about my upcoming trip, she stood up and announced that she was coming with me to Peru. She did, and I had the time of my life. Over the next two years, we traveled to Hong Kong, Beijing, Taiwan, Tibet and Bali, as well as throughout the United States.

What is the chance that two people living on opposite sides of the globe would ever meet? Would either of us have noticed the other if we had been immersed in our typical workday ritual? Would I have been so assertive to ask her not once, but twice, to join me, and would she have accepted, if either of us was not fully present?

From a pure statistical perspective, to have all these circumstances come together would have been virtually impossible. But the universe conspired to arrange these synchronicities, and we chose to recognize the opportunity and act by being in the present. Travel facilitates such moments.

While it is certainly possible and desirable to live in the present and experience unlimited synchronicities within our normal everyday lives, there are many times when we need a little boost. Consider taking a trip. Your life may change forever.

21

It's About the Journey

Nothing could embody the proverb, "it's not about the destination, it's about the journey," than our just completed, Sacred Journey to Peru.

Nothing could embody the proverb, "it's not about the destination, it's about the journey," than our recently completed, *Sacred Journey to Peru*. Everything about the trip was spectacular—the sights, the energy, the food, the environment, etc.—but what forever etched the trip into my mind were the experiences I shared along the way with the 17 explorers that comprised our group.

The magic began with our flight from Lima to Cusco. Just after we crested the Andes, I felt my crown chakra open up and lock into a group of "well wishers." This is different than the sensation you feel in your third eye when you sense someone on earth is trying to contact you.

I mentioned it to my seatmate, Leslie, who asked me how I could tell. I told her to place her hand 12 inches above my head. She shook her head in amazement at the heat; the energy was that strong. I knew this journey would be special.

Upon landing in Cusco, many of us were overwhelmed with feelings of joy, as evidenced by spontaneous outpourings of tears. Clearly, this was a homecoming. These feelings were even more pronounced at some of the sacred sites, especially the ones with formal, stone entrances.

Psychometry is the art of perceiving subtle energies in material objects by touching them. Stone entrances where thousands had passed over the centuries provided sensations that were stronger and much more tangible than holding a watch, for example. By placing our hands on these stones, many of us could perceive familiar sensations that welcomed us home.

In Cusco, due to a "miscommunication," a group of us had dinner together. As it turned out, there was no "miscommunication," as everything was in divine order. Had Jeannine listened more carefully, she would have joined a different group and missed contributing to our conversation.

During dinner, I recounted an incident that occurred a few weeks earlier, where a fellow I just met had a spontaneous past life recollection while sitting next to me at the counter of a Greek Diner. (He went so far as to begin shouting, "I can see the water. Can you see it?" which amused some of the patrons who were not used to people living in two different times at once.)

When I looked at Jeannine, I recognized her and said, "you were there, too, but you were a man back then." She nodded in acknowledgement and filled in more details, including the name of the city in which this occurred. Christine was also moved, as she remembered being rescued during the evacuation. Clearly, had Jeannine focused on the "destination," she would have missed the "journey" that included this recollection which gave us all goosebumps.

In many religious texts you read stories about "going up a mountain," or "going into the desert" to commune with God and gain inspiration. What the individual is doing is getting away from the "noise" of everyday life so that he or she can more easily use his or her inner senses to perceive the subtle vibrations of the inner worlds. Without the mental noise and the energetic congestion of radio, TV and cell phone transmissions, the sacred sites in Peru provided an ideal environment in which to meditate.

I looked for an opportunity to do so atop Machu Picchu during some free time and was joined by Christine, Kirsten and Leslie. Late in the day, the top of Machu Picchu was packed with tourists, photographers and guides speaking a variety of languages. I sat on a rock and attempted to meditate despite the distractions. I cleaned my psychic centers and raised my vibration to better attune with God, but kept getting the message, "wait."

Focused on my preparation, I didn't pay attention to what was happening around me. Without a word, my three companions had taken positions at the north, west and south of the terrace while dozens of onlookers simply vanished! In the silence atop the mountain, we had a beautiful meditation. As soon as we were done, the crowds returned.

While goals are critical to determining where you want to go, it's important to pay attention to the journey. From the mystic perspective, we are all destined to return to God, the Oneness. Were we only to consider the destination, there would be no time and space. There would be no experience of separation. And there would be no joy as you made a connection that brought you closer to God.

Our *Sacred Journey to Peru* was an opportunity to experience those little joys that better help us to connect with God. But you need not wait for a special trip to do this. Just contemplating the beauty of a flower or observing a child's joy at experiencing the ocean for the first time is part of the journey that you can savor forever, if you simply remember to do so.

22

A Lesson from Tibet

Our recent tour of Tibet proved, once again, that the universe is in divine order and that there are no accidents.

One of the hardest ideas for people to accept is that the universe is in divine order—that everything is exactly as it should be and there are no accidents. Theoretically, it's quite understandable, but to actually accept this principle is difficult. When things go wrong, it is almost human nature to look for someone or something to blame, especially when there is evidence to support your accusations. Yet, when this principle is embraced, and an effort is made to uncover the hidden lesson, your life may be enriched.

My girlfriend, Christine, and I had just come back from a 12-day tour of Tibet, that provided us and our fellow travelers with several opportunities to internalize this lesson. We joined a tour group from Taiwan comprised of Buddhist pilgrims, including two monks, who were seeking to visit many of the famous monasteries in Tibet, as well as experience the region's natural beauty. Only a few spoke English; the tour was conducted in Mandarin, with Christine translating for me.

Our tour operator, Chang, worked very hard to obtain all required permits and to keep things running smoothly. He told me that my application was particularly troublesome. It had been accepted, rejected and accepted on three successive days and my permit to enter the Potala Palace was not granted until the day before we were scheduled to visit. Despite his proven diligence, on three occasions he had me questioning his judgment.

On the first occasion Chang decided to take a shortcut to the desert monastery, Samye, to save 3 ½ hours of driving time. The shortcut required we conduct a 50-minute crossing of the

Yarlung Tsangpo River in a flat bottomed boat, followed by a 30-minute drive in the back of a modified pickup truck on a dirt road that resembled the surface of the moon.

The 13,000-foot altitude and the reflection of the sun off the water made the Tibetan sun extremely intense. Even more challenging was the truck ride, where dust and rocks buffeted us while we bounced over potholes the size of small school buses. One local who shared our ride almost got bounced out of the truck.

It would have been a simple task for Chang to tell everyone what to expect, but it didn't occur to this otherwise diligent operator. He apologized profusely, but several people were very upset.

The second occasion was the opening of the Shoton Festival, where over 300,000 celebrants from all over the world had gathered in Lhasa. At sunrise, monks unveil a huge thangka or scroll-painting of Shakyamuni (Guatama Buddha) on the side of the mountain. The brightly colored thangka only remains visible for a few hours before it is taken down and placed back in the monastery until the following year.

We boarded our tour bus at 5 AM, anticipating that we would be driven to the festival. Unexpectedly, the bus dropped us off two miles away; we had to walk up the mountain, at 12,000 feet altitude, to get to where we'd be able to see the unveiling. Part of the uphill journey was on paved roads, but the last portion was on dirt paths.

Again, it would have been a simple task for Chang to tell people what to expect and to wear proper footwear, but it didn't occur to him. Several people were forced to walk in flip-flops and casual shoes that were completely inappropriate for the terrain.

The third incident was our visit to Zhongshan Castle, overseeing the Palco Monastery. To get to this fortress, we had to climb up a winding road and several steel ladders to reach the top of the fortress, where we had a spectacular view of the nearby town and countryside. Again, Chang neglected to tell people what to expect.

I was puzzled. On the one hand, Chang had been extremely diligent in obtaining our permits and planning the most minute details of our activities, and yet, he had neglected to advise us of the obvious challenges we'd have to face.

Starting from the premise that everything is in perfect order, I tried to reconcile this inconsistency.

I realized that the people who were most inconvenienced were the ones that were most fearful of undertaking such activities. One woman admitted that after the boat and truck adventure she had unsuccessfully tried to call her husband hoping he'd be able to arrange an immediate flight back to Taiwan. She said that had she known what to expect, she would never have come.

But she did come. And both she and her friend discovered they had far greater reserves of strength and courage than they had ever imagined. They came away with an appreciation for their own physical strength, which had never before been tested. As she said after scaling the mountain to Zhongshan Castle, "I have the pictures to show my family. Otherwise, they'd never believe it."

It was not in Chang's nature to have shrewdly planned this outcome. He had revealed just enough information to attract the right people to the tour and yet been almost negligent in withholding key information to make the journey more manageable. He was no Machiavelli. Rather, he had acted as a channel for the universe to allow some people to experience and develop their own potential to a far greater degree than they ever would have. Those of us not physically challenged were not inconvenienced.

In hindsight, several people would not have gone on the tour had they known what to expect. And they would have lost out on, not only some spectacular scenery and historic sites, but rather, one of life's most precious gifts: a greater knowledge of themselves and their capabilities.

There are no accidents.

23

Practicing Psychometry in Tibet

Psychometry is the ability to sense subtle energy vibrations from material objects. Tuning into a piece of artwork can add "another dimension" to your appreciation of it.

Our recent trip to Tibet gave us an opportunity to practice a very useful mystic skill. Psychometry is the ability to sense subtle energy vibrations from material objects. Tuning into a piece of artwork can add "another dimension" to your appreciation of it.

Ever since the early 1900s, scientists have confirmed that everything is energy. Nobel Prize winner, Ernest Rutherford contributed the understanding that matter is mostly "empty space." Another Nobel Prize winner, Louis de Broglie, hypothesized that all matter has a wave-like nature, which was later proven. In 1982, French scientist Alain Aspect showed that information is somehow transferred at speeds beyond the speed of light, which violated one of Einstein's most fundamental axioms about our physical universe.

All these famous scientists confirmed what mystics have told us for centuries. "Everything is energy. You distinguish one substance from another by its rate of vibration or frequency." Mystics have also taught that much of the energy that affects our world is not perceivable by our simple objective senses. These influential energies can be of either higher or lower vibration. As examples, infrared radiation is below our visible threshold and x-rays are above it.

Each of our five objective senses, sight, hearing, taste, smell and touch, has a corresponding inner sense. The inner senses respond to vibrations that are much more subtle than physical vibrations. That is why when you meditate, you want to eliminate physical distractions, such as loud noises, bright lights, strong smells or unpleasant surroundings. Eliminating these helps you to to perceive the subtle vibrations, which are much higher and finer in vibration With practice, you can develop your inner senses and perceive phenomena beyond your objective senses.

Some people ridicule this idea, but remember, if you placed a person from the 18th century in any modern city today and told him that "invisible radio and TV" waves were passing through his body he would have also thought you were crazy.

The mystic practice of psychometry relies upon the use of your inner sense of touch or feeling. The simplest impressions you may receive are emotions, but the impressions may also come in the form of sounds, smells, tastes or images. We had many opportunities to practice in Tibet.

The Potala Palace, located in Lhasa, is the center of Tibetan government. It's 13 stories tall and appears even larger, having been built into the side of a mountain. It is divided into religious (red) and administrative (white) sections. I was eager to sense the vibrations within.

Upon entering the Potala Palace we were ushered into a waiting room. Only a certain number of people are allowed to visit each day and visitors are kept on tight schedules to ensure that the Palace does not get damaged. While waiting, I put my hands on the wall to sense the vibrations. Clearly, you could sense the love and devotion of the Tibetan people who had visited and worshiped at this site for over 1300 years.

As we got closer to the center of the Palace the feelings of love got stronger. There was no need to try and perceive the subtle emanations with my hands. The energy surrounded us. We passed by the rooms where the young Dalai Lama would receive his daily instruction. The strongest love vibrations were in the central temple in the heart of the Palace. This contained priceless relics, many made of gold, which is excellent at holding these subtle vibrations.

The Tibet Museum contains many ancient scriptures, tapestries, thangkas, statues and other works of art. The amount of love that went into each of these artifacts when they were created, as well as the appreciation of the observers that got to see, pray or chant in the presence of these works of art infused them with energy. This loving energy field was palpable and everyone in our group could sense it.

Many of the Tibetan monasteries in the area were also infused with this loving vibration. Our impressions varied in intensity, based on where in the monastery we were allowed to visit. One site with extremely strong energy was the Palco Monastery. We were allowed to listen to the monks chant and to take pictures. Dozens of orbs appeared in our pictures. (Not every monastery would let us take pictures.)

Another site with strong energy was at the Jokhang Monastery, the first Buddhist monastery in Tibet. We entered while several hundred people were worshiping. On the roof above, several dozen monks were praying, adding to the loving energy being generated.

At the Sakya Monastery, in Shigatse, everyone in our party was given a small bottle of "Tibetan Magic Water." This was the best tasting water that I've ever had. Clearly, the water was infused with the love of the monk's chanting and devotional practices.

While Tibet is a wonderful place to perceive these subtle vibrations, you can practice psychometry on your own, anywhere. One of the best ways is to exchange watches or rings with people in a group where everyone does not know each other very well. Watches or rings are especially good, as, typically, they've been in one person's possession for many years and so are thoroughly infused with that person's energy.

To get the clearest impressions, hold the object in your non-dominant hand, that is, if you're right handed, your left hand which will be more receptive. Close your eyes and tune into the object. Sometimes, asking yourself questions, such as "happy or sad", "positive of negative" can help you to focus. With practice you'll improve.

Metals hold vibrations very well. So do crystals. This may sound very airy-fairy, but if anyone ever pokes fun at you, you may remind them that our entire computer industry is dependent on the specific properties of quartz crystals. Even today, scientists are conducting advanced research on the use of quartz crystals to store information. Soon they'll discover what mystics already know, so get a head start and begin practicing psychometry today.

24

How to Relieve Stress

Understand how stress affects you and the ultimate way to prevent it from affecting your physical, emotional and mental health.

Stress is the result of outside stimuli pushing your mind, body or spirit out of balance. Adapting to new stimuli is how you increase your capabilities and develop new skills, i.e., the basis of growth. But, if the stimuli is too great or arrives so quickly that you are unable to adapt, then the resulting stress can lead to physical, emotional or mental problems.

Stress can be triggered by many factors, including: physical, emotional or mental abuse; life changing events such as a new job, moving, pregnancy or divorce; work or school-related deadlines; high stress occupations; and uncomfortable social situations.

Exposure to stress affects us in stages

In the first stage, when we experience stress, our bodies automatically react with the characteristic "fight or flight" response, also known as an adrenaline rush. In life threatening situations this is helpful, as adrenaline causes our bodies to increases our pulse, blood pressure and rate of breathing, better preparing us to do battle or to escape. When the outside stimuli disappear, often with a good night's sleep, we return to normal.

Continued exposure to stress, without a break, results **in the second stage**. In today's modern society, everyday stress from traffic jams, work, or just plain living, triggers this same reaction. We end up in a constant state of stress. We deplete our reserves, especially our adrenal glands, and lessen our ability to handle additional stress. Even our ability to sleep can be affected.

The final stage results from the accumulation of stress over time and leads to exhaustion. Unable to return our body, mind and spirit to its normal state of balance due to overwhelming stress, we suffer physical, emotional and mental breakdowns. Warning signs are: weight gain or loss, ulcers, indigestion, insomnia, depression, anxiety, fear, anger, inability to concentrate, moodiness, and other problems. It can be argued that all disease is a consequence of stress.

Aside from the practical steps of caring for yourself through eating and drinking sensibly, regular exercise, not taking drugs (whether legal or not), slowing down and cutting back on stressful activities, there is a more fundamental solution to coping with stress.

From the mystic perspective, and increasingly, the view of leading-edge physicists, everything is energy. You distinguish one thing from another by its rate of vibration. Physical matter vibrates at a lower frequency than emotions, which in turn are lower than thoughts. As majestic spiritual beings living a human existence, we have multiple bodies of increasingly higher vibration—our physical, emotion, mental and spiritual bodies.

Within each energy band, there are higher and lower vibrations. While stress can manifest physically, the underlying energies that cause stress are not physical. These dense, low-vibration, non-physical energies can lead to anxiety, fear or anger. *Unless you release the underlying energies, your health and, ultimately, your life will suffer*.

Whether or not you are able to cut back on stressful activities, your most fundamental step to eliminating stress is regular, direct contact with your innermost self. Communing daily offers you the opportunity to release stress.

Sleep is also beneficial, but when stress accumulates faster than it can be released, it's not enough. Even worse, chronic stress can adversely affect your sleep patterns rendering them ineffective in combating stress. Communing with your innermost self is your ideal course of action, which is best achieved through meditation. Regular contact with your innermost self will not only eliminate accumulated stress, but prepare you for future stress before it arises.

25

Overcoming Fear

Probably the most debilitating emotion that humans must confront is that of fear. You can eliminate fear by taking conscious action and being your true self.

Probably the most debilitating emotion that humans must confront is that of fear. Fear confuses. Fear paralyzes. Fear prevents you from thinking clearly, accessing your spiritual gifts and being who you truly are.

Fear is the anticipation of future pain. It's been said that 90% of humans are motivated to avoid pain, while only 10% seek pleasure. It's no surprise that we suffer from fear. We've been trained to fear from an early age. Don't play in traffic—fear of getting run over. Don't talk to strangers—fear of being abducted. Don't misbehave or Mommy won't love you—fear of abandonment.

As we grow older, we learn new fears: Fear of not being loved. Fear of being rejected. Fear of not having enough. Fear of being unworthy or inadequate. Fear of making a mistake. Fear of being restricted. Fear of getting fired. Fear of being annihilated by nuclear-armed terrorists.

Every day, we are bombarded with new fear-based messages by advertisers, politicians and the media. It's easy to understand why:

Fearful people are easy to control.

Fear is one of humanity's most primitive emotions, triggering the adrenaline rush associated with the fight or flight response to danger. In life-threatening situations, this is helpful, better preparing you to do battle or to escape. But in non-lethal situations, fear clouds judgment and encourages you to

76

REACT—rather than carefully consider alternatives—thus ensuring a less than optimal response to your problem.

Even worse, attachment to fear inhibits your ability to tap into your innermost self. Connecting with your inner master requires you to be balanced and your brain hemispheres be in synch. Fear causes your brain to automatically return to its dominant side—logical or emotional—again, ensuring unbalanced input into solving your problem.

Fear is a low vibration, dense emotion. Clinging to this negative, energy-draining emotion guarantees you will be unable to transcend to higher states of consciousness, characterized by higher vibration emotions such as love, joy, peace and happiness. You can't take your baggage to the higher worlds, so eliminating fear is critical.

All people, even warriors, have some degree of fear. What separates warriors from timid souls is not their inability to recognize danger. What makes some people warriors is their willingness to act in the face of fear. By repeated experience, warriors come to know that fear dissolves with conscious action.

Action has another benefit. It focuses you in the Now. By definition, fear is the anticipation of future pain, that is, FUTURE—not in the Now. Acting keeps you focused in the Now, which is how you reach higher states of consciousness— where time is malleable and fear does not exist.

As a 17-year old youth driving our family car with my new driver's license, I remember being threatened by a crazed driver on a deserted highway. It happened so quickly, I had no time to become fearful. Everything began moving in slow motion, giving me time to observe the situation. I had a bigger car, more horsepower and, if need be, I could run him off the road. I accelerated and left him behind. Only years later did I realize that by acting in the Now, time had stretched to assist me.

Look at your life and observe where you are stuck. Likely the cause is fear, in some form or another.

Ask yourself: What is the worst thing that can happen to you if you act and confront your fears? Will you look foolish? Will your self image suffer? Will you be rejected?

Recognize that all of these fears are ego-based. Your true self is not affected by any of these consequences.

In addition to dissolving fear and placing you in the Now, consciously choosing a course of action will take the focus off of you and your ego, and places it on the task at hand.

So what to do?

Begin simply by taking small steps. If you have a social anxiety disorder, you don't start to conquer your fear by signing up to address the UN. You begin by attending a meeting of people that share your interests. You don't even have to speak; just be there. If you immerse yourself in a subject that you love, you will lose yourself, you will have fun, and you will be in the Now, as you act or interact with others.

Remember, also, that failing to act will compound your problem. To protect your ego, you may come up with justifications for why you didn't do anything. You may convince yourself it was prudent, smart, unimportant, wouldn't matter, etc. Soon, you have convinced yourself that you did the "right" thing. This makes it harder to act in the future. Recognize that it is your ego that is busy justifying your inaction, not your true self. It is a self-reinforcing, bad habit you are developing.

You can nip this habit in the bud by bringing conscious awareness to your problem and then acting.

People that act in accord with their true self are not constrained by fear. They are not driven by their egos, and consequently are free to do what they like. These people are charismatic. They act from their innermost self. They are unconcerned with how others perceive them. They are not controlled by others. They are their own person, free to love and be loved.

The choice is yours. Love or Fear. Clarity or Confusion. Higher consciousness or stagnation. Eliminate fear by taking conscious action and being your true self.

26

Eliminating Anger

Anger is a mental quality that arises when expectations do not match reality. It cannot be eliminated by physical or mental means, but requires spiritual awareness.

After fear, anger is probably the next most debilitating emotion that humans must confront. Unlike fear, anger is a complex emotion. And unlike fear, which usually paralyzes, anger can spur you to take action, though not necessarily in a beneficial way. Reacting to anger-provoking events will usually make things worse.

If you analyze why you or anyone else ever gets angry, it's almost always because expectations did not match reality.

Here's a simple example: You order butter pecan ice cream from a Baskin Robbins store and they tell you they don't have any. You're angry. Why? Because you expected to get butter pecan ice cream from an ice cream store with 31 flavors, but the reality was they didn't have any.

Now, if you had ordered ice cream from a Starbucks and they told you they didn't have any, you wouldn't be so angry. Why? You still didn't get your ice cream, but since coffee shops don't generally serve ice cream, you wouldn't have expected to get any.

Not getting what you want by itself does not make you angry—only when your expectations are not met do you get angry.

Expectation is a quality of the mind. We have built up our expectations based upon our past experiences and how we've interpreted them. We then project these expectations into the future.

Consequently, anger is a quality of the mind. As such, "folk remedies" such as jumping, running or punching a bag or pillow will be largely ineffective. Following these suggestions will make you tired, but you'll still be angry. And yelling at people whenever you feel angry is also counterproductive. (Not to mention, increasing the likelihood of receiving a beating from people who don't appreciate getting yelled at.)

The pop psychology "let it out" anger reactions are also mostly unproductive. This is because as a mental quality, you cannot use lower vibrational, physical energy to diffuse your anger. As Einstein said, "No problem can be solved at the same level of consciousness that created it."

This means you can't use physical means, or even a mental means, to solve a mental problem.

You need to invoke a higher level of consciousness.

You need a spiritual approach.

What to do?

Immediately accept the reality of the situation and become fully present.

Only when you are present can you consciously decide if it's best to take action now or continue to accept the reality. Do not resist the reality. Your only two healthy choices are to act or to accept.

Complaining is nonacceptance, which will perpetuate your anger. It turns you into a victim, which the Law of Attraction tells us will bring you even more of the stuff you're complaining about.

Suppressing your anger is also nonacceptance. You still have your anger; you just buried it. It will still attract more anger, and, most likely, it will resurface when you least expect it.

You must act or accept.

Anger has no benefit, other than to tell you that you are acting unconsciously, that is, REACTING, based on habit or past experience. Getting angry is a habit that we all have experienced.

If you catch yourself, you have taken a step towards higher consciousness.

Here's a more specific example: You're attending your annual performance review. You did a great job for your company and expect a pay raise. You present all your accomplishments to your boss, pointing out the value you added to your company, and you request a raise. Your boss says "no."

What should you do?

Remember, act or accept. Anger has no place in this equation. You've already acted to give yourself the best chance for a raise. Further action, at this time, is not likely to change things. Given this, you must accept the situation completely and totally, without judgment or anger.

Assume that everything is exactly as it's supposed to be. You were not supposed to get a raise. The universe conspired to get you exactly what you and your higher self requested. This could be the stimulus to get you to take enlightened action in another direction. You will want to meditate and figure out what that is. Then you can choose to act consciously to create the preferred reality that matches what you want.

This may involve updating your resume and networking with industry contacts for a new job. Or it may involve working on plans for your own business. In either case, taking conscious action will uplift you. You will be amazed at the amount of abuse you can tolerate, when you know that the situation is only temporary because you are taking action to create the reality that you want. You don't even have to tell anyone else; all you need to know is that you are taking enlightened action. Your spirit will soar.

The fundamental principle at work here is that you are not your mind. Since expectations are creations of the mind, they are not needed. Your true self is beyond the mind.

In a longer term course of action, you will want to dis-identify from or eliminate the thoughts and emotions lodged in your energy bodies that are framing your expectations. In many cases, these thoughts, feelings and beliefs are not even yours! They were instilled in you by your parents, teachers, religious leaders, peers, co-workers, bosses, the media, etc. You accepted them and they are framing your experience of reality today.

When you recognize this is what's happening, you will more easily release them. One of the best ways to do this is while meditating; by being fully present with the single-minded intention to clear them from your being.

27

Dis-Identifying from Your Emotions

Presence and purification are two spiritual practices that lead to dis-identification with your emotions and thoughts, which helps you to connect to your true self.

As our last chapter explained, anger arises when expectations do not match reality. Saying "I am angry," is one of the most disempowering phrases you can ever utter. Not only does saying it deny the reality of the situation, more dangerously, using the word "AM" equates an emotion with who you are. This is a surefire path to suffering.

The ego is responsible for misleading you into identifying yourself with your body, emotions and thoughts. You may *have* a body, *feel* emotions and *think* thoughts, but none of these are who you *are*. You are a magnificent spiritual being. Identifying with anything other than your true spiritual nature will eventually lead to suffering.

In his latest book, *A New Earth*, Eckhart Tolle defines the "pain-body" as "the energy field of old but very-much-alive emotion that lives in almost every human being." It contains both individual and collective elements. In other words, this is your emotional body, which contains all the accumulated emotions and feelings that you have become attached to. For all of us that are not yet self-realized, this emotional body becomes a pain-body that is activated by various stimuli.

Identification with your pain-body can totally blind you to your true self. In some cases when your pain-body is activated, your personality can change overnight as you forget who you are and become your pain. The Law of Attraction tells us this is a self-reinforcing cycle. Pain attracts more pain and when the conscious mind is contributing, your pain-body grows even faster.

If you suffered from a bad experience in the past, whenever a similar experience arises, your pain-body automatically recalls the memory. Instantly, it reminds you of this by secreting the same chemicals that produced the initial feeling, just like a tuning fork that begins to vibrate when a nearby turning fork plays the same note.

Worse, you get addicted to these chemicals, even when they're not good for you, which reinvigorates your pain-body.

Your goal is to break your identification with your pain-body, and identify with your true self. There are two practices that can help you to accomplish this.

Presence

The first is to bring present awareness to the situation. This is in keeping with the mystic directive, "know thyself." When you are aware that you are being triggered, rather than simply reacting, you can remain detached, and separate your emotions from your true self.

Tolle believes you will eventually become so sick and tired of being stimulated by your own and other's pain-bodies that you will, in desperation, seek to dis-identify with them. This can happen in an instant, since all that's needed is to shine present awareness on the situation.

This is what happened to him, and explains the revelations that others undergo, when they "snap" from overwhelming suffering and spontaneously gain Presence. The downside of relying on overwhelming suffering is that it can take a while to get "fed up," and "snapping" does not always produce a positive result.

Purification

The second approach is the path of purification, that is, eliminating the negative energies that are lodged in your emotional body. This also requires present awareness, but can be dramatically facilitated by an external source of high-vibrational energy.

Physics tells us that higher frequency energy is more powerful than lower-frequency energy. When you infuse higher dimensional energy into a lower dimensional form, the lower energies must leave or be transformed.

By eliminating the lower density, negative energies, you will not be stimulated by another's pain-body. Your tolerance will grow exponentially, as you will no longer unconsciously resonate with others' emotional pains. You will remain compassionate but detached.

Of course, without changing your thoughts or, at least, becoming aware of the thoughts that precipitated the painful emotions, clearing out your pain-body will be only a temporary solution. But when your emotional body is cleared, you will be less likely to identify with it. Unhealthy feelings will become the exception, rather than the rule. You will come to identify with your true self vs. your emotions.

When your emotional body is clear, the Law of Attraction will work in your favor. People that were previously attracted to the emotional pains in your energy body will no longer be attracted. Purification eliminates the toxins that attract "toxic people." When this pain is replaced by love and higher vibrational energies, you will attract higher minded, spiritual people and will actually repel angry or fearful people.

As Jesus said, "For he that hath, to him shall be given: and he that hath not, from him shall be taken even that which he hath." This is the Law of Attraction in biblical terms. You must decide what you want to attract. Presence and purification lead to identification with your true self; unconscious thoughts lead to pain and suffering.

28

Taking Back Your Power

You have been trained from birth to give away your power to "experts." It is not only your right, but your responsibility, to decide, for yourself, what you think and take back your power.

Lately, I've been watching episodes from the 1970s TV show, **Kung Fu**, on DVD. It starred David Carradine as Kwai Chang Caine, a half-Chinese, half-American Shaolin priest who wanders the post-civil war American West looking for his long-lost brother.

Caine is a martial arts master who resorts to using his fighting skills only when someone's safety is at stake. **Kung Fu** introduced many Westerners to some of the basic tenets of Eastern thought. Like fine art and true wisdom, many of the teachings espoused in the show are timeless and universal in nature.

One of my favorite episodes, *El Brujo*, concerned an evil witch who was terrorizing a small town. The townspeople so feared this man that they willingly gave away their power—performing whatever actions he demanded—hoping to please him. At one point, the townspeople were resigned to letting an infant die because the evil man had cursed the baby.

When Caine arrives, he cures the infant using herbs. Later, the witch curses one of the town's leaders, condemning the man to death in 24 hours. As before, the leader tries to give away his power—this time, pleading for Caine to rescue him. Caine simply replies, "Why do you believe him?"

The leader's shock matches the shock I sometimes see on people's faces when I ask them the same question, after they report "news" they've seen on TV. The number of people who willingly accept the thoughts and edicts of others, without question, is astounding, but understandable. In our society, we have been trained since birth to delegate our thinking and give away our power to outside "experts."

When you spill hot coffee on yourself, you are advised to hire an attorney to argue that you were not warned the coffee was hot. When you watch a political debate, experts come on later to "explain to you" what you just heard and what it means, as though you were incapable of forming your own opinion. You are taught to blindly allow doctors to pump drugs into your body, and to ignore the wisdom contained within your own self.

While soliciting outside advice can be helpful, blindly accepting another's thoughts, without discernment, violates your responsibility to yourself as a majestic spiritual being living on earth.

In the **Kung Fu** episode, a flashback to Caine's early training at the Shaolin monastery in China echoes this simple truth. His blind teacher, Master Po, explains, "The undiscerning mind is like the root of a tree—it absorbs equally all that it touches—even the poison that would kill it."

Caine chooses not to accept the poison. When the witch curses Caine, nothing happens, for the simple reason that Caine "does not believe him." The witch's hold over the town immediately vanishes.

So it is today. You need not blindly accept whatever fate or expectation your parents, siblings, teachers, political leaders, media commentators, friends or co-workers have dictated for you. You not only have the right, but the responsibility, to decide, for yourself, what you think.

To do so, you must become aware of your thoughts. You may well discover that the majority of thoughts that you think every day are not even your own. You may further discover that many of these thoughts are disempowering, intended to induce fear or otherwise direct your behavior.

You did not incarnate on earth to "play it safe" or be a robot that simply "follows the rules, hoping to fit in." You were created in the image of God. This means you were born to create. Your life's mission is to tap into your inner self and express the wisdom from within—not to blindly accept the viewpoint or doctrine of some expert, guru or societal program as the default setting.

Understand that as a creator, every thought you think is creating your world. Will it be a prison ... or will it be a heavenly garden? Wouldn't you rather be the architect of a beautiful paradise worthy of such creative power?

To create "Heaven on Earth," you must regularly tap into your divine nature by whatever name you choose to call it: master within, higher self, inner light, etc. When you tap into your inner self on a daily basis, you begin to assume and deepen your majestic spiritual nature.

There is no other mission on earth as critical as learning to tap into your inner self for guidance and expressing your inner light. As numerous spiritual traditions assert, "The highest and best source of wisdom comes from within." Learning to ask for, listen to and accept this guidance is essential to developing spiritually.

When you have tapped into your inner self, you then can use your mind to interpret the "voice" of your inner master, and take inspired action to create or express yourself—whether you are writing, painting, singing, working, playing or simply thinking.

Now, be forewarned: there are those who may tell you that relying on your "mind" is dangerous—that doing so is egotistical. Some "schools" of thought actually argue humans think too much and, to balance this tendency, they should rely more on emotion and instinct. This "theory" misses the point entirely. The issue is not whether you, or anyone else, thinks too much, but rather WHAT VOICE DO YOU LISTEN TO—the voice of your ego or that of your higher self?

Experience, intuition and certain other clues will help you to recognize the voice of your inner self and avoid the pitfalls of the ego. (We will cover this subject in more depth in our next chapter.)

Until then, it's time to think your own thoughts and take back your power!

29

Listening to Your Inner Master

Learning to distinguish between the voice of your ego and that of your inner master or higher self can be tricky. Here's how to tell.

In our last chapter, we discussed your spiritual responsibility to take back your power—to think your own thoughts and avoid blindly accepting the edicts and opinions of others. The ability to think is a God-given gift that humans enjoy. By tapping into your inner master and interpreting the intuitions that you receive, you are using this gift for its highest purpose. The tricky part is distinguishing the voice of your inner master (or higher self) from the voice of your ego.

In our society, we have been conditioned to accept our ego as our true self. ***Revolver***, a recent film directed by Guy Ritchie and starring Jason Statham, makes this point precisely. It's a bit hard to understand, until you realize that the "enemy" referred to in the movie is the ego.

Initially, ***Revolver*** appears to be a gangster's tale of revenge. Jake Green is guided by two "wise" loan sharks who offer to teach him how to win the ultimate game. They offer cryptic clues like, "The greatest enemy will hide in the last place you will ever look." Jake assumes that it's an external enemy who is attempting to subdue him.

It's the same for most of us. We look outside ourselves at our potential "enemies," vowing to overcome them. In reality, everything that we perceive in the world is just the outer reflection of our inner thoughts. ***The ultimate battle lies within***.

Our ego is designed to protect us from harm. As more attention is directed towards it, it grows. It is not necessarily an enemy, as ***Revolver*** portrays it, but can better be likened to an unruly child who wants what it wants, when it wants.

Just like an unruly child, the ego must be guided by a wiser being, that is, your inner master or higher self. A necessary step on the spiritual path is the surrender of the ego—that is, listening to the voice of your inner master, not your ego.

In **Revolver**, Jake is told, "You've heard that voice for so long, you believe it to be you," and "the greatest con that he ever pulled was making you believe that he is you." He begins to realize the battle is within him.

At the film's climax, the camera cuts between "true Jake" and "ego Jake." Finally, Jake tells his ego, "You don't control me. I control you." He has won the ultimate game.

So it is in real life. When you can distinguish between the voice of the ego and that of your inner master/higher self, and then act based on the wisdom you receive from your inner master, you are well on your way to winning the ultimate game.

A long-term mystic once said, "Don't let your mind act as the attorney for your ego." When you are busy "convincing yourself" that you are right, you're using your mind as an attorney. It might be logical, but it's not your highest source of wisdom.

So, how to tell the difference?

The voice of the ego is characterized by being: self-centered, self-aggrandizing, fear-based, angry, anxious, rationalizing, complaining, and reactive.

Conversely, the voice of your higher self is characterized by being: humble, loving, compassionate, peaceful, harmonious, trusting, tolerant, merciful, forgiving, grateful and proactive.

Every moment of every day, you make a choice to listen to either your ego or your higher self.

The more you identify with your higher self, the greater your spiritual power—the faster things manifest—the more synchronicities you experience. Ultimately, you merge with your higher self and become Self-realized.

On earth, the "game" is rigged to give your ego the edge. It takes clarity, desire and dedication to change this default setting, to listen to your higher self.

The best time to perceive the finer, more subtle voice of your higher self is during meditation, when your external senses are shut down. I would never consider making an important decision without meditating, or as one wise guru stated, "go to the market without first going to the bank."

With practice, your inner voice will become louder. You will "feel" or "intuit" that certain actions are best, rather than having to solely rely on your intellect, which, ultimately, can't know all there is to know to make a truly "perfect" decision.

You will know that you've had a breakthrough when you contemplate a situation that seems totally contradictory, but then it suddenly makes sense. The flash of enlightenment that reconciles two seemingly opposite viewpoints is joyful. Zen masters give their students koans, or riddles, to encourage these experiences.

Another sign that you are listening to your inner self, is when the answer you receive makes sense on more than one level. Real truth reveals itself in many ways.

Whatever your preferred spiritual approach, practice listening to your own inner master to manifest your true self.

30

Being Yourself

The simple advice, "Just be yourself," contains a nugget of profound wisdom that goes far beyond attracting money, fame or love. "Being yourself" is your one and only mission on earth.

How many times have you felt anxious when you were required to face a stressful situation, such as interviewing for a new job, speaking in public, or going on a date with a prospective new love interest?

And how many times, when you asked your closest friends or mentors for advice, did they try to allay your fears by telling you, "Don't worry—just be yourself."

Probably, your friends meant:

- You're a good candidate for this position and are fully qualified for the job;
- You have lots of valuable information to share that your audience will appreciate; or
- You are a fun-loving person who your date will enjoy.

And your friends may be completely correct.

But even deeper, the simple advice, "Just be yourself," contains a nugget of profound wisdom that goes far beyond attracting money, fame or love. "Being yourself" is your one and only mission on earth.

As we discussed in an earlier chapter, *Taking Back Your Power*, you were created in the image of God. This means you were born to create. Your life's mission is to tap into your inner self and express the wisdom that lies within—that is, Be Yourself.

This is not easy. In today's world, you are continually conditioned to define yourself by a number of external, superficial characteristics, such as your: name, age, gender, race, nationality, occupation, religious affiliation, marital status, familial relationship, political party, economic status, educational degree, or other such label.

And if everyday language is not already limiting enough, there's a whole list of acronyms to further define you: SWF—Single, White, Female or DINKS—Dual Income, No Kids.

All such names or acronyms are inherently limiting. You are a majestic spiritual being experiencing life on earth with a body, heart and mind.

So how do you "Be yourself"?

One self-realized sage, Nisargadatta Maharaj, taught that the best way to learn to be yourself is to first recognize what you are not. His teachings are simple, devoid of religious jargon or dogma. He believed that in order to help anyone, in order to change the world, you must first know who you are. Many of his discussions would begin with "Do you know who you are?"

People would fumble around trying to answer the question, not quite knowing how to answer.

What he taught is that you are beyond your body, beyond your heart, beyond your mind, beyond even consciousness; you are the witness that sees yourself seeing, that perceives yourself perceiving.

You are the apex of the "I" ... which leads in to who you *truly* are—the Oneness that mystics seek.

Clearly, you are not any of the superficial things we mentioned earlier.

- You are not your body. After all, who is directing your body?
- You are not your emotions. For who is feeling these emotions?
- You are not your mind. For who is thinking these thoughts?

Nisargadatta taught that all attempts to limit or define yourself lead to conflict. Definitions based on your own memories are needlessly repetitive and limiting. When you know who you are, you can transcend your limitations, including your past, and be a true Creator. Self-realization is primarily the knowledge of this conditioning, i.e., the mystic's goal "to know thyself."

In the mystic world, all is One. There is nothing outside of the One. There is only the One thing.

Now, you know that you exist. And you cannot ever *not* exist.

So, knowing that there is only the One thing and that you *do* exist, there is only one logical conclusion:

The One thing is *us*, that which exists as us ... the knower, the thinker, the perceiver ... is the divine aspect in all of us.

When we keep contemplating, "Who am I?" we go all the way back to the beginning, to the essence, to the innermost self. Then we realize that we are all the One.

When you tap into that innermost self, there is no stress. There is nothing that is needed. When you act, directed by your inner voice, you are aligned with your highest purpose and you will automatically do what is best in any circumstance.

This may involve "chopping wood and carrying water," as the Zen proverb advises. Or cutting out extraneous activities that do not provide spiritual nourishment. The seemingly tumultuous times that we are entering will encourage more people to go within and seek out their true purpose in life.

So, as the flawed institutions crumble around you, as more horror stories appear daily on the "news," remember, everything is unfolding according to a divine plan. Everything is exactly as it should be. You are a magnificent spiritual being. Listen to your inner voice and "be yourself."

31

Escaping the Matrix

Escaping the Matrix is a metaphor for the mystic path of enlightenment. Understanding the rules that govern the Matrix provides you with a way out of suffering and towards a life of bliss.

The Matrix was one of the most popular and thought-provoking movies of all time. Viewers all over the world were captivated by the film's primary message: People get into deep trouble when they mistake what they *perceive* for *reality*.

What most viewers do not realize is that prior to the release of this groundbreaking film, western intelligence agencies were already using the term "the Matrix" to describe today's world. This was in contrast to their work with remote viewers, who would "escape the matrix" to gather intelligence. Art truly does imitate life.

In the movie, the Matrix is an elaborate Artificial Intelligence computer simulation that's so captivating that people mistake it for reality. People perceive they are walking about and interacting with others, but their physical bodies are actually submerged in fluid-filled pods, "plugged into" the Matrix, while their vital life force is harnessed to power the Matrix.

After Neo (Keanu Reaves) learns the truth, with the help of Morpheus's (Lawrence Fishburne) training, he is able to overcome his misconception that the Matrix is reality. Neo rebels against the machines that create his false reality and, eventually, he escapes the limitations of the Matrix. To others, he has developed superhuman abilities, but, "in reality," he has merely recognized the truth.

Escaping the Matrix is a metaphor for the mystic path to enlightenment.

The Matrix can be defined as the world that we perceive, which includes the physical world, as well as higher planes of emotions and thoughts, which also affect us.

Within the Matrix, are countless fear-based thoughts and emotions that condition us to accept limitations. We are taught that we have little power, and what little power we do have, we are advised to delegate to authority figures and experts. Swimming in a sea of negative thoughts, we are prompted to use our creative ability to imagine even more negative thoughts. Without introspection, the Matrix gets darker and more dense.

Anyone who blindly accepts these prevalent, negative thoughts will have his or her life path dictated by the Matrix.

But those who recognize that it is our collective thoughts and beliefs that power the Matrix will recognize the way out.

When we incarnate on earth, we temporarily forget the higher truth of who we are. Our life mission is to remember, to connect with our innermost self, so that we may transcend the Matrix.

The reality we perceive with our senses is not the true reality, but merely a small portion of reality, masquerading as the whole. But, unlike the "alternate reality" that Neo must extricate himself from, in our "reality," there is no need to rebel. Rather, our goal should be to transcend. We want to "be in this world, but not of it."

The outer world is a reflection of our inner thoughts and beliefs, whether individual or collective, which have been conditioned by our experience in the Matrix. Consequently, the Matrix is a learning environment, where we get feedback on how our thoughts manifest. Thankfully, our negative thoughts do not (typically) manifest instantaneously. Otherwise, we would risk the spontaneous destruction of our world by thinking negative thoughts.

Clearing yourself of negative energies through daily meditation can provide a direct link to the "ultimate reality," i.e., the pure consciousness residing within each of us. As your negative beliefs are purified through regular contact with the "light" of your divine nature, unhealthy emotions, such as fear and anger, will naturally begin to diminish, and you'll be free to transcend to higher states of consciousness. You will "download" more of your own true self, while simultaneously and automatically attracting others of similar vibration.

Your world will become more synchronistic. You will repel angry, fearful people, and those who stick around will become calmer and more centered. You will radiate love. By simply **being** in higher consciousness, you will have a greater effect on the world than the most gifted orators and political leaders.

The higher your consciousness and energy are vibrating, the faster your thoughts will manifest. When you align with your innermost self, you are aligned more closely with the Source of all creation. At the apex of your individual consciousness, you are connected with The One. You then have at your disposal the entire universe to help you manifest the highest good for all.

In actuality, we are single points of awareness in the Oneness that is Reality. What we interpret as the physical world is the projection of this awareness, which is taking place in the Mind of God. We are, as Shakespeare pointed out, merely "actors" in a divine play.

When we wake up to this knowledge, the play does not stop. We are free to act or interact, in bliss and peace, unattached to the Matrix. We have within us the power to create "heaven on earth."

In the past several chapters, I have described various methods you can use to release fear, eliminate anger, dis-identify with your emotions, take back your power, listen to your inner master, and be yourself. The goal of all of these exercises is the same: to help you escape the Matrix.

32

Alchemy Revisited

Alchemy is the process of replacing or transmuting lower, negative vibrational energies with higher, positive ones—at every level of your existence—body, mind and spirit. Here are some tips.

As I wrote in an earlier chapter, *Mental Alchemy*:

Back in the Middle Ages, alchemists sought to transform base metal into gold. They searched for an elusive substance, the philosopher's stone, which would bring about this conversion, known as alchemy. But to initiates of the ancient mystery schools, alchemy was primarily an allegory for the real work of spiritual and mental alchemy.

Mental alchemy is the process of transmuting your thoughts to improve your life and expand your mind, while spiritual alchemy is the never-ending process of transmuting a soul personality from a less refined one into a more refined one.

As we know, everything is energy—everything vibrates. The difference between one substance and another is based on its rate of vibration. Thoughts, feelings and beliefs also vibrate. As a spiritual being, you also vibrate and exist on many levels.

Alchemy is the process of replacing or transmuting lower, negative vibrational energies with higher, positive ones—at every level of your existence—body, mind and spirit.

When you understand this principle, you can take the proper action for any circumstance at every level: physical, emotional, mental and spiritual.

Physical

A wide variety of physical stimuli and sensory input can affect your being.

Are you filling your body with artificial sweeteners, fake fats, junk food and other toxins? Do you subject your objective senses to a non-stop barrage of mainstream news and fear-based content? Do you surround yourself with negative people that take pleasure in tearing you down?

When your boat is taking on water, it's much more effective to stop drilling holes in the hull and patch them up, before you begin baling out the water. This means, stop filling your physical environment with negative, draining energies.

Now, it's true that these thoughts and beliefs will still exist in our world, but by turning off your TV, you can, at least, shut the door to the non-stop reinforcement of these energy-sapping thoughts. And it's also true that spiritual power can offset base thoughts, but why expend any energy undoing something that can be fixed by the simple physical action of turning off your TV?

A critical time for rejuvenating yourself is just before retiring for the night. Don't watch the news before going to bed. Instead, consider reading an uplifting book or listening to relaxing music. You can also meditate and visualize how tomorrow will be even better. When you go to bed, give yourself the best possible chance for renewal, especially if it's not practical to take the other physical actions recommended to minimize negativity.

Emotional

Scientists and philosophers have debated for centuries whether emotions are caused by thoughts or simply the result of physiological processes. From the mystic perspective of wholeness, the answer is BOTH! To transmute negative emotions, we must also address physical and mental causes.

Mood swings often result from poor eating habits, which can be addressed at the physical level. Dwelling on past hurts and traumas re-energizes negative emotions. Releasing these via forgiveness or acceptance replaces negative emotions with the higher emotions of love and compassion. Other emotions such as anger have a mental cause (when expectations do not match reality) and must be addressed at the mental level.

Mental

The Law of Attraction tells us that we attract experiences that match our beliefs. With few exceptions, the energies that you attract will influence your vibration. It is a self-reinforcing cycle.

So while your beliefs will lead you to "see what you believe," they can be changed. By replacing limiting beliefs that are hindering your development with positive ones, you can transform your life for the better. A powerful technique is described in the earlier chapter, *Mental Alchemy.*

To ensure a never-ending source of positive thoughts that will raise the vibrations of your thoughts, you must tap into a higher source than your conscious mind. The ideal source is your own inner master or higher self.

Spiritual

Every decision you make is based either on your ego or your higher self. *Spiritual alchemy is therefore the process of incorporating more and more of your higher self into your life decisions.*

When you align with your higher self, your energy and the power of your intent increases. This is a positive, self-reinforcing cycle that leads to mastery and self-realization.

When you tap into your innermost self and radiate that energy, you are no longer as influenced by external energies. You are freer to live a life of Heaven on Earth. And, having tapped into the ultimate energy source, you can help others to connect with their own divine power. You are not only improving your life, but the world as a whole.

If your goal is to lead the most joyful, empowered life possible, then your choice is simple. Employ alchemy at every level of your life for both personal and global transformation.

33

The Eagle and the Grasshopper

When the student is ready, the teacher will appear.

Once upon a time there was a grasshopper, who through diligent practice became one of the best hoppers in the land. She loved hopping so much, she began teaching other grasshoppers how to hop. She was very disciplined and required they faithfully follow her commands. She told her students what to eat, when to eat and how to eat. During their practice sessions, she barked out orders telling them exactly what to do.

Soon, baby grasshoppers that had never hopped before were learning how to hop, adults that could barely hop were hopping much better, and even those who already were good hoppers could now hop much higher. The teacher felt very fulfilled.

Then one day a creature showed up that she had never seen before—an eagle. She was determined to teach the eagle how to hop, as she was certain that hopping was the path to fulfillment and enlightenment. But every time she approached the eagle, he just said, "There is no need." She kept trying, but the eagle insisted, "There is no need." Finally, at a large gathering of all the grasshoppers, she pointed to the eagle and announced angrily, "No matter what I say or do, this stupid eagle will never learn how to hop. He does not understand us."

The eagle looked at the grasshoppers and said, "You are content with hopping, but I can fly."

"Stop this foolish talk of flying!" screamed the teacher. "Flying is just imagination and fantasy." She turned to the grasshoppers and said, "Any time such thoughts arise, immediately focus your energy back on your hopping—this is how you will become enlightened."

"You know nothing about flying!" said the eagle with a commanding voice that silenced the grasshopper. The eagle turned to the grasshoppers. "I can show you a world far beyond your grass fields. If you listen to me, I will teach you all to fly."

The eagle waited for them to respond, but when he looked around, incredibly, all he saw were blank looks on the faces of the grasshoppers. He walked away, very sad.

Later that day, while soaring far above the tall grass of the fields, an insight emerged from deep within the eagle's innermost being. He realized that to communicate with the grasshoppers, he would have to speak the grasshopper's language—the language of hopping.

The next day, the eagle returned to the grasshoppers' world and began hopping with them. The grasshoppers were surprised. Not only could the eagle hop, but he could hop as well as any of them.

The teacher kept a wary eye on the eagle. She feared her grasshoppers would get swept away by the eagle's stories.

But the grasshoppers were curious and some of them began to sneak away to talk to the eagle. "How is it that you know how to hop and yet you talk of flying? It goes against our teacher's orders."

"Hopping is useful, but when you can fly, it is no longer necessary."

"Tell us more," said the grasshoppers.

The eagle began describing the world beyond the grass fields, a world that included mountains, rivers and oceans. He sensed they were nervous but assured them was nothing to fear.

The grasshoppers asked, "What's it like to fly?"

"When you are flying, you are totally at peace. Sometimes, I feel like I am connected with everything and watch as everything happens automatically without any effort on my part. I am no longer an eagle flying, but I become flying itself."

Later that day, a solitary, brave grasshopper approached the eagle and asked, "Can you take me flying?"

The eagle nodded and gently took the grasshopper in his powerful talon. With a few beats of his wings they were aloft.

Circling overhead, the grasshopper could see the mountains, rivers and ocean that the eagle had described, far beyond the familiar grass fields. Careful not to go too high, the eagle soon returned the grasshopper to the ground.

Hearing the commotion, the other grasshoppers rushed over to find out what had happened.

"He took me flying!" announced the brave grasshopper proudly, but then admitted, "I got dizzy. I didn't like it."

"But our teacher has told us that flying is just imagination." said another grasshopper.

"Bless your teacher and be grateful to her, for she has taught you to hop," said the eagle. "But now you know the truth."

The eagle looked deep within the eyes of the brave grasshopper. Though she was still a bit dizzy, he saw a spark within her very being. He looked at the others and saw that the spark was already spreading to them. Soon, they would no longer be content with just hopping—they would all want to fly.

"My work here is done," announced the eagle abruptly. "Some day you will all learn to fly!"

"But if you leave, who will teach us?"

"Rest assured, as it has always been, when the student is ready, the teacher will appear."

With that, the eagle unveiled his powerful wings and soared off into the sky.

34

More Synchronicities

Synchronicities may lead you to your life's calling.

When I originally published *The Eagle and the Grass-hopper* in my newsletter, I sparked quite a few responses from readers that experienced unusual "coincidences" just before or after reading it. Readers emailed me stories of people soaring down mountains using special winged clothing, a grasshopper that hitched a 20-mile ride on an automobile and an international businessman, who told his new acquaintance, nervous that no one would able to guide her after he left, "Don't worry. When the student is ready, the teacher will appear."

As I wrote in an earlier chapter on meaningful coincidences, or synchronicities:

Recognize whenever you are "in the flow" and take note of your thoughts and what you are doing. At the least, this is what you were meant to be doing at that particular moment in time. If you see a pattern, recognize that these thoughts and actions may be your life's work.

A few years ago, an amazing synchronicity-filled weekend convinced me to spend more time writing on mystical subjects. My book **Mystic Warrior** had been released and I was looking for conferences attended by open-minded people that would welcome the idea that, not only are humans capable of far greater things than most people can conceive, but that advanced mystic skills like telepathy, remote viewing and precognition were being used today.

I received an email that a ***What the Bleep Do We Know*** conference would be held in Santa Monica, California. It would bring together the scientists, spiritual teachers, filmmakers and lead actress featured in the movie in one setting for lectures, questions, and discussions. Even better, there would be vendor booths available.

Three weeks before the conference, I called the vendor organizer, Gloria, to inquire about a booth. She told me the price was $1200 a booth. Quickly, I calculated that I would have to sell nearly a hundred books just to cover the cost of my booth—and that was without taking the costs of airfare, hotel and the program into consideration. In any case it didn't matter. Gloria then told me that all vendor booths were sold out and the waiting list for booths had 34 names on it already. There was no way I would ever get a booth.

Without the possibility of defraying some of my costs with book sales, I debated if it would still be worth attending. I figured I could distribute flyers and make some contacts at the show. Still, with my estimated expenses of $250 airfare, $450 hotel, and $395 program, it was going to cost me over $1000 to attend.

That was when my friend Curtis called. He lived nearby in Florida, but "coincidentally" he was visiting his brother, who lived in Santa Monica—a five minute walk from the conference. He invited me to visit. His offer saved me $450 right off the top.

After buying a non-refundable airline ticket for $250, all I needed was to buy a program ticket, which, I figured, could wait.

Two days before the conference another email arrived—the program was completely sold out. I tried to call the conference organizers to beg for a ticket, but they were out of town.

With my plane ticket and a place to stay already in hand, I figured it would be worth the risk to see if they could squeeze me in. I packed 12 books and a ream of color flyers into a box and left for LA.

At the conference the next morning, I tracked down Gloria to ask, "Where's the literature table? I need a place for my flyers."

"There is no literature table," she answered.

"I flew here all the way from Ft. Lauderdale. I couldn't get a vendor booth and two days ago, I found out that tickets are sold out. Surely, there must be some way I can, at least, hand out flyers?"

She remembered my call about a vendor booth, looked at me, as if to size me up, and then commanded, "Follow me."

She led me to the vendor area and stopped at a table in the rear, in front of a huge window overlooking the Pacific Ocean. She asked the husband-wife team setting up their booth, "Would you mind giving this gentleman a 2-foot section at the end of your second table so he can display his book?"

The woman, who looked somewhat familiar, asked, "What's the name of the book?"

"*Mystic Warrior*."

The woman smiled and said, "That's where I know you. I got a copy of *Mystic Warrior* from you at the INATS convention in Orlando. I loved it. Sure, you can set up at the end of our table."

I thanked them profusely. "Fantastic," I thought. The only thing I needed to make the conference complete, would be a chance to hear a few of the speakers—five in particular. I went to the registration table to see if there were any cancellations. The woman handing out the badges said, "No, but you can purchase 'standing room only' tickets to any of the lectures for $20 apiece." Instead of paying $395 for the entire program, it would only cost $100 for my five favorite speakers.

During the conference, at my improvised, 2-foot booth, with only my book and a stack of flyers to display, I sold all the books I brought and took orders for a two dozen more. I spoke with dozens of fascinating people and 116 attendees signed up for my newsletter. I was extremely grateful.

Clearly, this was not something I could have planned. The universe had conspired to make it possible and provide me with what I needed. These synchronicities had confirmed that I was on the right path.

Similarly, be alert to synchronicities that appear in your own life. Recognize that you attracted them with your thoughts, feelings and beliefs, and that the universe provided you with what you requested. Pay close attention—your life's work may be calling!

35

Manifestation and Synchronicity

Several, highly improbable synchronistic events provide a key insight into the process of manifestation.

For the past two months, I've been on an "extended visit" to the Santa Monica area. I began by visiting my friend, Danielle. During this time, I've experienced a number of synchronicities that were so unlikely, they seemed to defy the laws of probability.

What I've come to realize is that, while they **were** highly improbable, such synchronistic events are entirely consistent with the universal laws of manifestation.

Three Synchronicities

To get a deeper appreciation of this, let's look at a few examples. Upon arriving in Santa Monica, I shared a table with a fellow at Whole Foods while eating lunch. That evening, coincidentally, he walked into the local alehouse, where I happened to be enjoying a fine beer. I told him he reminded me of an artist I had met a year earlier in Venice. It turned out that they were roommates.

On another occasion, I was looking for the phone number of a massage therapist, whose card I had lost. Two hours later, I was able to make an appointment when I ran into her at a food co-op that I had never previously visited.

Back at that same alehouse, I met Bill, a man who was familiar with many of the spiritual subjects I've written about and who had read 2/3 of the books on my Recommended Reading list at the back of my novel, **Mystic Warrior**. Two days after our initial meeting, he called to tell me that another fellow who saw us talking had asked him, "Who was that guy?"

Bill told me that he replied, "Remember that book I told you to read some time ago, *The Secret Teachings of All Ages* by Manly Hall? Well, Ed knows a lot of that stuff; so pay attention when he speaks."

I thanked Bill for such a nice compliment. Manly Hall is a "major-league mystic." His book is encyclopedic in its treatment of symbolism and imagery.

Then I started to think, "I'd better brush up on my Secret Teachings, since I've got some high expectations to meet." Unfortunately, my own copy was back in Florida.

The next day, my friend Danielle handed me a book and said, "This book's a little too dense for my tastes, but I figured you'd like it."

As you can guess, the book was Manly Hall's, *The Secret Teachings of All Ages*.

Invitations Arrive "On Cue"

Not wanting to overstay my welcome, I told Danielle I'd like to find another place to live. Soon afterward, I began getting invitations to housesit and dog-sit for other families in the area.

It was uncanny how one gig would end and another would begin *on the exact same day*. On *three* occasions, I picked up my old "landlord" at the airport and dropped myself off at my new place on the way back.

In one case, I was scheduled to move into a new house on Friday, the same day my current landlord, John, was scheduled to return from Colorado. On Wednesday, my new landlords called to say they wanted to leave a day earlier. "Could you care for our dogs starting tomorrow, in addition to John's dog?" they asked.

I readily agreed. Less than an hour later, John called to say he was coming back a day earlier. Without any effort on my part, the universe had already lined up my next home, while simultaneously supporting my efforts to help others.

A Key Insight Into Manifestation

Knowing this, I was still curious as to what was causing my thoughts to manifest so quickly. Manifestation involves bringing your well-formed blueprint or thought-form into physical form. The clarity and intensity with which you hold the finished item in your mind's eye largely determines the speed at which something will manifest. An enlightened master can do it instantaneously. For the rest of us, there's a lag.

I contemplated this question while meditating, and received an illuminating "reply." An image of a huge, well-stocked department store formed in my mind's eye. Following that was an image of a small country store that only had the bare necessities on its shelves.

Clearly, both urban and rural environments have their advantages and disadvantages. Being isolated in a rural environment, free of distracting thoughts, is conducive to connecting with your inner master. However, what occurred to me is that being surrounded by like-minded people in a compact, urban environment can aid in the process of manifestation.

Prior to my staying in Santa Monica, I'd been living in a much less populated town along Florida's Gulf Coast. There, while I'd experienced similar synchronistic occurrences, they would typically happen with less frequency and not normally in such rapid succession.

In a high-population area like Santa Monica/Los Angeles, whatever you're desiring or intending is likely to align with the desires or intentions of at least someone or some group of individuals; that is, some of these like-minded thoughts are floating around in the ethers, partially manifested, awaiting the energy and/or clarity to manifest.

So, in the case of my having numerous synchronistic events and desires manifest over a short period of time, rather, than having to start from scratch, I was "piggybacking" atop many similar thoughts, which sped up the process.

Here's an analogy: Rather than having to build a home starting with a forest full of trees, as in a rural environment, there's a huge inventory of homes already existing in an urban environment. In both cases, you can manifest a home; but having a ready supply of potential homes will speed up the process.

A Reminder about Abundance

My experiences reminded me of another important lesson about abundance. One of the places I stayed on three separate occasions is half a block from the Pacific Ocean. It would have been unaffordable if I had to rent or buy it. But while I'm staying there, I'm getting the same benefit as if I owned the property.

Similarly, this past weekend, as I cruised through Malibu Canyon driving a new Audi A4 sedan, I was reminded that even though it was not "my car," I was experiencing the exact same joy traversing the beautiful landscape as would the owner.

From a spiritual viewpoint, the only benefit to "owning" an object is for the experience it can provide. If you have access to the experience, then, you have abundance. Expressing your gratitude for these abundant experiences tells the universe you want more of them.

And as far as I can tell, it's working!

36

Love, Anger and Manifestation

My friend's recent dating adventures illustrate several spiritual principles that are important to bear in mind, especially concerning matters of the heart.

The past two weeks, I've been visiting my friend, Danielle, in Santa Monica, CA. She had recently ended a relationship and was busy dating. Her experiences dramatically illustrate several spiritual principles that I've previously written about.

Danielle complained to me that while the man she was dating was fun and interesting, he wasn't very attentive. Days would go by without any contact. I suggested that "he's just not that into you," as the recent movie suggested.

She agreed.

I asked her, "What is it you really want?" As I've written before, this is the first step to manifestation.

She wrote out a list. At the top, she wrote, "I'm dating a man who adores me and wants to spend time with me."

I also suggested she check in with Roberta, a mutual friend of ours, who is highly intuitive.

Roberta told Danielle that she would soon attract a man who would "sweep her off her feet—just like in the movies." Danielle added that description to her list.

Two days later, Danielle had a first date with a new prospect, Todd. Within an hour he had told her, "You're the woman I've been waiting for all my life. Now that I've found you, I won't ever let you go. No matter what happens, I will be your friend for ever."

When the flower girl asked, "Would he like to buy a rose for the lady?" Todd bought all 14 of her remaining roses and presented them to Danielle.

A friend of Danielle's happened to be in the restaurant and told her the next day, "it was just like a movie."

Danielle had manifested exactly what she had envisioned, but she was a little concerned. She asked me if I felt her new friend was sincere. It was a little "over the top."

I suggested she stay positive and move forward, but proceed cautiously before jumping in with her heart. Yes, I felt he was sincere, but my concern was whether he would be just as sincere a week later in professing his undying love for some new woman.

Danielle was smitten, however. Todd had told her he would be out of town for a week and for the next three days, he texted her messages every few hours. He told her he would fly Danielle and her daughter to wherever he was working so he could spend more time with her. He made plans to see her as soon as he returned that Saturday. Danielle made him a gift for his upcoming birthday.

On the fourth day, Danielle received no texts or calls. On the fifth day, she got a text from Todd saying he would not likely be in the LA area for the next six months and that she should not expect to see him much.

Danielle was angry and actually surprised at how angry she was. After all, she had only had one date with Todd and had known him for less than a week. I was sympathetic while sharing my observation that "reality did not meet her expectations." At the least, she expected to have a second date with the man who "had waited for her his entire life," but the reality was that he was not available.

"Even worse," I said, "you're angry at yourself because right from the start you were hesitant, but you allowed yourself to raise your expectations. When your new, higher expectations were not met, you became livid."

Again, she agreed.

We re-read Danielle's list that described her ideal man. Without prompting, she gasped and said, "I never specifically asked for someone who was available—just someone who would want to spend time with me!"

Danielle revised her list to include that the man was available. Nothing else changed. She still envisioned someone who would want to sweep her off her feet—just like in the movies.

The next day she drove into the parking lot at the local market. Before she could even put up her car window, a man came over, looked into her eyes and told her, "I just have to tell you this. You are absolutely gorgeous."

She smiled and thanked him, as he slowly walked away.

When she returned to her car, she found his card with a handwritten-note on the back under her wiper. "I'd like to get to know you. Please call or text me."

Danielle did. She has already met Jake for several dates already.

He has all the qualities she listed—and he's available.

This mini-drama demonstrated the importance of getting clear on exactly what you want. It also showed the role of anger in alerting you when expectations are not matching reality. In both instances, if you're not getting what you want, you'll have to take corrective action.

That's what Danielle did. Instead of reacting by pining away, hoping her unavailable man would suddenly appear or sulking at her misfortune, she modified her request to the universe. The universe responded by creating the desired reality she was seeking.

This is taking enlightened action. This is what we should all strive to do.

37

The Science of Intention

The universe arranged a powerful demonstration of Intention for my skeptical friend, Ron, reminding him, "what you put your attention on grows."

Last month, I visited southern Oregon. I anticipated a quiet retreat in the woods, while I tended an old friend's house, located an hour outside Ashland. Instead, I played a role in an "intention experiment," which rewired some brain synapses in my friend, Ron, and which again demonstrated "there are no coincidences."

For a variety of reasons, Ron's initial plan for a month-long pilgrimage to India and his subsequent plan to go on a road trip to Texas were both derailed. The universe had arranged for us to spend some time together, with no cell phone service and no high speed internet.

For years, Ron has been a video technician who's been living almost as a recluse. He was eager to talk to someone, but most of what he shared could be labeled "negative." He'd had a number of experiences that "taught" him people were either selfish or naïve—especially women. Ironically, what he most wanted was a long-term relationship with a woman.

I tried to get him to change his attitude, but he was not listening. Thankfully, the universe arranged for him to see how intention works.

A Series of Coincidences

One evening, when he was heading to a class at a local university, I asked him to drop me off at the local tavern. He cautioned me, "You'll be bored silly. All you'll meet are miners and loggers."

I said, "Don't worry—I won't be bored."

Two hours later, he came in to find a pilot sitting next to me, entertaining me with tales of flying over the north pole. Ron was surprised at my "luck," but attributed it to "coincidence."

A few days later, I told him I wanted to find out what was happening in Ashland.

Ron sent me to do research at a coffee shop which had high speed internet access.

My intention was immediately rewarded. I was greeted by Donna, who had "coincidentally" stopped in for a quick cup of coffee before she headed back to Ashland.

When Donna found out I had arranged to do a talk at the Metaphysical Library and was eager to learn about Ashland's many events, she pressed the speed dial on her phone, handed it to me and announced, "Johnny runs the Ashland Resource Center. He'll tell you what's happening in Ashland and how to promote your event."

That evening, I told Ron of my "coincidental" meeting. Again, he was surprised.

I told him I wanted to spend some time in Ashland. Ron warned me that that "the people there are ungrounded and flighty, and many of the women hate men."

I said, "I have no intention of meeting any man-hating women."

He explained, "Based on my experience, that's what you're likely to find."

"That's because that's what you expect. I don't expect that."

He said, "Look. If you start with a box of predominantly blue marbles, even if there are a few red marbles, chances are you're going to pick a blue one. I'm just telling you this, so you're not disappointed when you get to Ashland."

I replied, "First of all, people are not one-dimensional marbles. Second, you are assuming that the universe is a mechanistic system, which totally discounts the role of consciousness and intention in your experience."

He said, "It's just a statistical fact."

I said, "That's completely wrong. That's 19th century science; that's not how the universe works."

I decided to make it more personal. "You told me you'd like to get remarried, but everything you're doing is sabotaging your efforts to achieving that goal."

He couldn't argue with that.

"Even if you think I'm completely wrong, why not try it for 30 days and see what happens?"

Ron was near tears. "I know you're trying to help me, but it's not easy."

"Just watch your thoughts. Every time a **negative** thought comes into your head, notice it, and start thinking about something else that's **positive**. And if you want to meet a woman, start talking to them, **with the expectation that they will want to hear from you**."

Ron agreed to try my proposal. A week went by. His negative rantings diminished; and when he did start in on one, he would quickly catch himself and say, "In the past, x-y-z happened; but now ..."

I moved into downtown Ashland and agreed to keep in touch with Ron, to continue sharing our experiences.

With my new friend, Johnny's help, I was meeting movie producers, internet marketing gurus, advertising mavens, public relations experts, tantric practitioners, healers and writers, all of whom welcomed me to Ashland—exactly as I expected.

There are two aspects to setting an intention:

Clarity - The reason most people's lives are so chaotic is that their thoughts are chaotic. When you are constantly sending out mixed signals, it should come as no surprise when the universe responds with apparent randomness. Clarity turns diffuse lighting into a coherent laser beam.

Emotion - Emotion is the energizing force to your thoughts. If you're lukewarm on your intention, you will get lukewarm results. If you're passionate about something, it's more likely to manifest in the form of vital, dynamic results.

After I returned to Santa Monica, I called Ron.

I could hear his excitement over the phone. He had approached a woman he was interested in and she asked him to work with her on a video project. He was amazed how his new attitude and expectation were working.

It's too early to tell if Ron's new approach will stick. It's easy to relapse into comfortable, but unproductive habits. So far, though, the initial results are promising.

It's important to remember the ancient wisdom, "What you put your attention on grows." Observe your thoughts. When you catch yourself thinking negative thoughts, change them. So, simple, yet so profound, this is the essence of the Science of Intention.

38

Relationships and Heartbreak

Conflicts that arise within a love relationship, and even the end of a relationship, can provide us with opportunities that can further propel us towards spiritual mastery.

Susan, a recently divorced "friend of a friend," is coming to terms with the fact that her life has changed dramatically, since her husband of 21 years left her. There are two aspects of her experience that are instructive for anyone who is, or has recently been, in a relationship.

The first is how one deals with the inevitable conflicts that will arise in a love relationship (no matter how "healthy" that relationship may be). The second is how one deals with the heartbreak that will likely arise if and when a love relationship ends.

The Relationship Crucible

Relationships are one of life's greatest pleasures. They are also one of life's greatest classrooms. While our hearts are filled with love and affection, our intimate relationships naturally provide us with tests and trials—sometimes on a daily basis—to help us grow more masterful in our spirituality. Relationships act as a crucible, in which to draw out any "flaws" and bring them to the surface for our purification and spiritual growth.

With a casual friend, you can overlook minor annoyances or idiosyncrasies. With a live-in partner, they must be faced. The successful resolution of a conflict can bring you closer to your partner and increase intimacy. Both partners grow as a result of facing and overcoming these obstacles.

When seen in this light, you can choose to view a difficulty that may arise between you and your love partner as an opportunity to grow, and work to overcome it. But, if one or both partners are unwilling to look within and do a little self inquiry, the growth will stop and so will the benefits of the relationship. Not everyone is ready or willing to undertake such self inquiry.

This is not to say that you should break up, get divorced or abandon your commitments, just because of some "roadblock" that's arisen in your relationship. Every effort should be made to work things out—to compromise, make concessions and fulfill your obligations, while remaining true to your core values.

But ultimately, your mission on earth is to listen to your inner master, develop yourself, and share your gifts with the world. And while it's almost always more fun when you have a partner, if that partner is actively discouraging your personal and spiritual growth, you may have to end the relationship ... *or it may end for you*.

As Susan reflected on her marriage, she was forced to examine several unattractive aspects of her marriage that she had previously ignored. Had she and her husband addressed them early on, they might have been able to overcome them. After evaluating their options, it became clear that divorce was the best alternative for both of them.

Even knowing this, Susan is heartbroken and has become distrustful of men. Despite her pain, she must accept that the universe has conspired to advance her spiritual evolution. So must anyone who has ever suffered from heartbreak.

Heartbreak

In all breakups, the person with whom you shared your love is gone. You are no longer the focus of his or her attention. And, almost always, you feel a hole in your heart.

Heartbreak teaches us compassion and forgiveness—how to be gentle with others, knowing how acts of mistrust or betrayal can hurt us deeply, and how forgiving ourselves and others can bring us to greater self-awareness. Compassion and forgiveness are qualities that humanity is cultivating.

If your partner leaves you, it would be wise to wish him or her well, knowing he or she may not be ready for the intensity of self inquiry and consequent growth that a profound relationship can entail.

When you no longer have your partner showering you with love and affection, you may be tempted to either find an immediate replacement (usually a bad idea) or be forced to go within, at least temporarily, and seek an even deeper level of love.

As you open your heart, go within, and incorporate higher vibrations of love into your being, you may still feel just as pained that your lover has abandoned you or ended the relationship. The difference is that you will recover much faster, for you will have a reservoir of love that you can tap into to ease the "temporary shortage."

We are not required to have a relationship, in order to access the love that we all seek. Neither is it necessary to become a monk or a nun.

Ideally, you are connected with your innermost self, tapping into that infinite reservoir of love, and sharing it with a partner who is similarly attuned. You are both contributing to a loving environment, in which you are both fully accepted and encouraged to be yourselves. This is the blueprint for a true spiritual marriage, where you and your partner can both realize your full spiritual potential.

Susan is talented, smart and attractive. If she uses her divorce as an opportunity to go within and tap into her inner self, in time, she will overcome her mistrust of men and connect with someone with whom she can share her newfound insights, compassion and independence. Conversely, she can choose to blame her "ex" for all her troubles, act like a victim, attract more untrustworthy men to confirm her belief, and block further spiritual growth.

This is true of all relationships. As Socrates said, "The unexamined life is not worth living." When conflicts are used as an opportunity for self inquiry, with an eye towards spiritual purification, even the end of a relationship can provide us with experience and compassion that can further propel us towards spiritual mastery.

39

Intimacy

Intimacy cannot be purchased or bartered for sex. On the contrary, it can be offered freely, without cost, and is a path to fulfillment.

Recently, a very attractive woman, Jennifer, told me that one of her greatest fears was that she would have sexual relations with a man and that he would then abandon her. She wanted a life partner, but based on her fear and her actions, I could see that she was inviting the very behavior she feared most. In my experience, this is quite common.

Jennifer's behavior was similar to that of a Swedish woman I met ten years ago and that of an actress I met this summer. All three women had been conditioned to use their beauty to get what they wanted—offering the promise of future sex in return for things and experiences they wanted now. However, this reliance upon the body—and ultimately, the ego's idea of fulfillment—is a recipe for disappointment, if not misery.

Men frequently sabotage themselves in a different way. They have been conditioned to equate their "net worth" with their "self worth," and will often use money to get what they want. They will buy their date gifts or take them to fancy restaurants in the hopes that their date will reciprocate with sex. This approach may eventually result in temporarily satisfaction; but, again, this reliance upon one's financial wealth—and ultimately, the ego's idea of fulfillment—will not get them what they truly want.

What both men and women really want is intimacy. It cannot be purchased or bartered for sex. On the contrary, it can be offered freely, without cost, and is a path to fulfillment.

The verb "intimate" means "to make known." When you are physically intimate with your partner, you are obviously "making known" the physicality of your body. But "intimacy" is not limited merely to the physical dimension. Intimacy is a "making known" of who you are on every level: physical, emotional, mental and spiritual. It is a state of being fully present with another. It is a willingness to be completely honest; literally, to "bare your soul." Intimacy means being yourself.

When a man or woman feels safe and secure, he or she can be his or herself. Amma, the hugging saint from India, came to Los Angeles this past summer. She embodies nurturing, loving energies. Her event was an ideal setting to meet and see people as they truly are.

The actress I met there seemed to be open, spontaneous and fun. Early on, she revealed that she had never had a love relationship last more than six months. One week later, she was fearful and calculating, while dropping sexual hints of "things to come." When I pointed out the mixed signals she was sending, she exploded, completely unwilling to look at her behavior with any degree of objectivity.

In her view, here was another man who did not meet her expectations. In my view, here was a woman destined to repeat her experience of dissatisfaction, since she refused to take responsibility for the lack of intimacy in her life and was attempting to use her physical attributes to attain emotional and spiritual wholeness.

My Swedish friend would dress suggestively and use sexual innuendoes (including physical touch) to hint at "things to come." Energetically, she could withhold or unleash her kundalini energy at will. Often she would do so when there was little chance of physical intimacy, such as in a public place or when I had to be somewhere else.

If the "on again, off again, maybe I will, maybe I won't" behavior continues in an emerging relationship, even after sexual relations, most men will disappear and the woman will have "proven" once again that men are "only after one thing and must guard it to avoid being abandoned." This is a type of conditional love, which is a barrier to intimacy.

Men are equally guilty. Aside from not sharing their feelings, they will often encourage this "barter economy" by implying that they have invested sufficiently to get the promised rewards. This makes a woman feel like a commodity (or worse). Both of these behaviors act to block intimacy.

Intimacy does not mean sleeping with someone before you are comfortable (if ever) or throwing money and gifts at them to show you care. It is being open and giving of yourself. There is nothing more charismatic than a person who radiates his or her true essence.

Energetically, your openness with your partner can be felt (and seen by those who are clairvoyant) by the opening of the chakras, or energy centers. In general, the more that are open, the greater the potential connection with your partner.

When all your chakras are open, especially your heart and crown chakra (pineal gland), you can more easily attune with God/the Universe/the One. You are connected with who you truly are and, consequently, you are "intimate with yourself." Then, you are more fully "ready" to be intimate with your partner. Even better, you have much more to share.

When this is the case, there is no overwhelming biological imperative to seek out a partner. You are already feeling complete. Your desire in finding a partner, then, arises from the natural impulse to share your "completeness" and to deepen it, by merging your energy with your partner's.

It is our spiritual destiny to be intimate with others and with ourselves. So rather than trying to buy or trade for what is your birthright, just be yourself.

40

Sacred Sex

Sacred Sex can improve our health, strengthen our energy bodies, help manifest our heart's desires, with the ultimate goal of communing with God.

To many people, the words sacred and sex do not belong in the same sentence. To others they may imply sex used for purposes of procreation. To the mystic, sacred sex is a way to improve our health, strengthen our energy bodies and help manifest our heart's desires, with the ultimate goal of communing with God.

Human sexual energy is among the most potent energies found on earth. The drive to mate is innate in human beings. Marketers use this drive to sell just about every product imaginable, from luxury goods to simple grooming items. You do not have to be a marketing wizard to recognize a long sports car sliding on a rain-slicked road hints at the sexual satisfaction you will derive from owning that vehicle.

The Law of the Triangle states that when two opposing energies come together, there is the potential to create a third energy. When a man and a woman come together, the potential is to create a child. But this energy can be used to manifest **whatever** you desire, as well as to commune with God.

Kundalini energy is the name given to this energy that usually lays dormant at the base of the spine. Upon activation by yoga, breathing exercises, meditation, natural spiritual development, or by a partner whose kundalini has already awakened, it rises along the spine through two channels called nadis. Like two intertwined snakes, the energy crosses at each of the lower six chakras. The seventh chakra represents enlightenment. The medical caduceus, the symbol of the

American Medical Association, is a graphic representation of kundalini energy rising.

In many sexual encounters, only the lower two chakras are involved. This can produce a brief flash of pleasure followed by a void because the other chakras are not involved. It can be tiring, as the sexual energy has been disbursed. Sleep often follows such encounters.

On the other hand, when a man and a woman engage in foreplay as a part of a sacred sexual experience, they act as catalysts for each other, encouraging the energy to rise in their partner. Over time, and sometimes spontaneously, this energy releases blocks in the chakras and burns off impurities in your energy bodies. As the energy rises, it is possible for both men and woman to experience multiple orgasms. Distinctions between male and female can disappear and the identification of whose orgasm is being experienced becomes blurred, as the two partners become one.

Far more sexual energy is produced by such an encounter, and aside from the obvious potential for pleasure, sacred sex strengthens the etheric body and opens passages to higher consciousness. The etheric body contains the blueprint for your physical body. A stronger etheric body can improve your health, while magnifying your desires and increasing the likelihood of their manifestation. This is especially true for thoughts you hold at the point of orgasm.

For best results, a woman must feel completely safe, loved and protected in order to release fully the energy contained within her being. This is an understandable basis for certain religious beliefs that people should only have sex within the context of marriage. The issue is not whether you have a society-approved license, but that the woman feels loved, protected and adored.

Sexual energy can also be produced by same sex relationships or by an individual alone, but in these cases you don't have the opposite polarities or the mixing of the male/female hormones and body fluids that augments the energy and brings it to its fullest expression.

Remember, each sexual encounter results in a transfer of energy. You want to be careful as to what and whose energy you're taking into your own energy bodies. Negative or low vibration energies are not conducive to becoming enlightened and will inhibit your getting closer to God. These low energies merely add to the discordant energies that must be burned off if you are seeking spiritual advancement. This is even truer for women as they are the receptacle for the male's energy.

In a committed relationship the two partners act as mirrors for each other, intensifying the purification process. The goal of our spiritual evolution is to eliminate all impurities from our energy bodies. Sacred sex intensifies the process and allows couples to eliminate the negative, while experiencing higher levels of consciousness than either partner could attain on his or her own.

When all the benefits are considered: improved health, release of impurities, strengthened etheric bodies to manifest your desires, not to mention the pleasure derived, it's a wonder more people do not pursue this ecstatic activity. Especially, when it contributes to our ultimate goal of communing with God.

41

The Soul of a Bicycle

An "evolving" bicycle is the perfect metaphor for life on earth and our ultimate quest to "know thyself."

When I was in high school, I was crazy about bicycles. My friends and I would take day-long bicycle trips to explore the far reaches of Long Island, often riding 60 miles or so in a single day. My bicycle was my vehicle to see the world.

Years later, when I moved to Florida, I bought a top-of-the-line Panasonic bicycle from a local bike shop that was going out of business. The frame's steel tubing was so thin and light that it "pinged" when you flicked it with your finger.

Right away, I updated some of the components. I replaced the old rat-trap pedals with modern clipless ones, replaced the chainrings, put on a different seat that better fit me, and added a micro-adjusting seat post. I began riding every morning up and down A1A, the road which runs along the ocean in South Florida.

Over time, I would replace the parts that wore out, like the tires, chain and brake pads, and my rear derailleur, which cracked. Whenever I had a chance, I would upgrade the components. I got a set of brakes from a riding buddy who won them in a race, aerodynamic wheels from a bike shop having a "blow-out" sale, and handlebars from a friend who didn't like their anatomical shape.

My riding turned into training. On weekends, I would hook up with a pack of racers who sped up A1A every day. My biggest thrill was keeping up with the pack on Saturdays, which was the most intense day, when they dropped all the "pretenders."

Unfortunately, the humidity of Florida is toxic to steel frames. The brazings that held the brake cables rusted off. I had a professional frame builder strip the frame, repaint it in the red and yellow Coors Light team colors and braze on new fittings. Even with the new paint job, the frame developed a rust spot, which eventually wore through the ultra-thin steel tubing.

I bought a Trek aluminum frame from my same riding buddy. I transferred all the components from my steel frame to the new one and adjusted everything, so it fit me perfectly.

As I looked at my bike, I realized that, over time, *every single component*, including the frame*, **had been replaced**, except one—the crank arms, which never wear out. It happened so gradually, though, that it was always "my bike."

And then I realized that this is a perfect metaphor for what happens to our bodies. Every component or cell in my body is replaced as it wears out, and yet it's always "my body."

Your body's components are made of the food you eat; so if you want to keep them in peak condition, you'll want to eat healthy, natural foods in the right proportions. Exposure to toxic environments—whether physical, mental or spiritual—also speeds up the wear and tear of your body's components; so you'll want to surround yourself with positive, uplifting energies, whenever possible.

We are reminded, here, of the timeless teaching: "You are not your body." Your body is just the vehicle for your soul to experience the world, just as my bicycle was a vehicle for me to experience the world. Even though the body's appearance changes over time (and over lifetimes), the soul is eternal.

Further reflection on the question, "Who am I?" will remind you that "You are not your emotions" and "You are not your thoughts," both of which come and go.

You are a majestic, spiritual being, which has a body, feels emotions and thinks thoughts. Ultimately, as you keep on contemplating, going deeper and deeper into your innermost self, you connect with the Divine aspect, or soul, at the core of every one of us.

We are all animated by this same Divine aspect. We are each single points of awareness in the Oneness, from which all else springs. We are all destined to merge with this Oneness and experience the world in total bliss.

As we each move towards this state, known as enlightenment, illumination or self-realization, we receive clues from our innermost self, or soul, that guide us forward. In general, when we follow these intuitions, we experience joy and meaning in our lives.

My bicycle is in storage back in Florida. I'm going to have it shipped to me in California. I am quite certain its "soul" would want to experience life in Santa Monica.

42

A Lesson Inspired by the Tour de France

"Do what you say you're going to do" is a profound bit of wisdom that is more than just a way to increase your chances for success—it should be a way of life.

The Tour de France—the word's most prestigious bicycling race—is being held this month. It brings back memories of my days of racing bicycles when I was younger. Besides the miles and hours I spent training, I used to read everything I could from top coaches and cyclists about how I could become the best rider I could be.

One article contained a bit of advice that I especially treasured. It was an interview of Mike Walden, a legendary coach who trained many national champions and Olympians. Something he said conveyed a universal truth, which I appreciate even more today for its profound wisdom.

Mike had a rule: "If you say you're going to ride 'x' number of miles, then you must ride that number of miles. If you're not feeling well or don't have the time, then commit to riding less miles; but whatever the number of miles you commit to, you must finish."

His logic was simple. You are developing habits when you train. You want to develop the habit of perseverance, not quitting.

But beyond developing good habits, his "rule" contains some sage advice. In short, he is saying, "Always do what you say you're going to do." (Or as Don Miguel Ruiz stated in his bestseller, *The Four Agreements*, "Be impeccable with your word.")

What's profound about this?

Your every word, your every thought, your every utterance is a commandment to the universe. The universe is conspiring to make every one of your pronouncements come true. Why would you ever want to turn yourself into a "liar" by not following through on your pronouncement?

It's not wise to promise something and then not deliver. This can be devastating to your business career, as, after all, your reputation is built on your ability to keep commitments. But it can have equally bad consequences at home.

For example, say you tell your young son that you'll read him a bedtime story; but then you get engrossed in some movie or ballgame on TV and put him off. You have just announced that your words mean nothing—to both your son and the universe.

Beware the ego

Whether it's greed, pride, the desire to be liked or some other "ego-driven" reason, you may be tempted to "inflate your importance" by promising something you can't deliver. Yes, this is the ego in action. You might have every intention of delivering it when you make your commitment, but then you realize it might be time-consuming, costly, or inconvenient, so you drop it.

Worse, when confronted, you may try to justify your position, by reframing your original promise: "I didn't really mean it," or "I meant that only if such and such happened," or you blame some third party. As a long-term mystic once advised me, "Never let your mind act as an attorney for your ego."

If you make a commitment, you must follow through. And don't wait until those who "owe" you follow through on their commitments. You don't want to slow down your own progress, while you wait for others to "catch up."

Act now, not later

I have a friend who complains that people she relies upon do not follow through on their commitments. In a conversation, I pointed out that she didn't follow through on some of her commitments. I asked her, "How can you expect people to follow through on their commitments, when you don't follow through on yours?"

She "explained" that she will start following through when they do.

I told her she is giving them way too much power. "Why would you knowingly put your life on hold, and place that kind of power in the hands of such irresponsible people?"

Every time you say you're going to do something and don't do it, you're announcing to the universe that honoring your commitments is not important. This is **not** a habit you want to cultivate.

What happens when there's something you really want to manifest?

If you've already built up a track record of making announcements that never come to pass because you've been out of integrity with your words and actions, then, when you want to manifest something important, it's going to be more difficult. After all, based on your past performance, you have little reason to believe anything will happen, so how likely is it to manifest?

This is not to say that you should "play it safe" and never aim for goals that are slightly "out of reach," so as to avoid failure from not following through. You owe it to yourself to strive for greatness by expressing your true inner essence.

What it means is that if you DO commit to something, you do everything in your power to attain it. And if you fail, you get up and try again. The lives of all winners are littered with temporary setbacks and failures. And every one of these successful men and women started with the principle of doing what you say you're going to do.

Integrity and enlightenment

For reasons beyond just increasing your chances of success, doing what you say you're going to do should be a way of life.

Your objective is to have your thoughts, words and deeds in perfect synchrony; that is, you don't lie—you act with integrity. But, this means more than just being honest and moral. Integrity also means being whole and undivided. It's a step toward merging with the Oneness, which represents our ultimate goal—enlightenment.

Conclusion

Whether your goal is to be the best bike racer, teacher, parent or business person you can be, or whether it's to attain our ultimate goal of enlightenment, start by doing what you say you're going to do.

43

The Mechanic

When your mind is open and you approach every experience as an opportunity to learn, even a "less-than-honest" car mechanic can teach you valuable lessons.

What can a "less-than-honest" car mechanic teach us about spiritual evolution and improving our lives?

A few months ago, my Honda Accord developed an oil leak. My long-time, trusted mechanic had recently retired so I was forced to find a new one.

A business associate, Ken, recommended Dan and led me to his garage so I could drop off my car. There was very little activity at the garage and my intuition told me something was wrong. Dan explained that he had just come back from a long vacation and he hadn't yet notified his "regular" customers. This meant he'd be able to fix my car promptly. I disregarded my intuition and left my car with him.

After keeping my car for an extra day "to make absolutely sure he repaired the leak," Dan presented me with an astronomical bill. In addition to replacing the normal seals and gaskets prescribed by standard maintenance, Dan explained that my leak required replacing an $8 seal, but since it was buried in the heart of my car's engine, it required 8 hours of additional labor. Because he "liked me," he was only going to charge me for 6 hours, which at $75 per hour meant an additional $450 dollars on top of the $300 normal maintenance bill.

I doubted his truthfulness but since I had not asked for an estimate and had no way of checking his story, I paid the bill. When I started my car, the engine warning light came on. Dan plugged his portable computer into my car and announced I needed a new sensor. He told me to bring it back tomorrow and he'd repair it.

As someone once said, "I was born, but it wasn't yesterday."

The next day I brought my car to the Honda dealership. The mechanic showed me where a circuit had been unplugged. His puzzled look spoke volumes as he tried to figure out how it could have happened. He plugged it back in and the problem disappeared.

Again, there was no proof that Dan had intentionally disconnected the circuit, but I vowed never to go back to him. I relayed my experience to Ken, advising him to find a new mechanic.

Last week, Ken told me his BMW had an oil leak and asked me to give him a ride to his mechanic—Dan.

I reminded him of my experience and pointed out alternatives: there were 10 other garages, as well as the local BMW dealership, all within two miles of Dan's garage.

Still he wanted to return to Dan's.

I warned him to get an estimate and be especially leery if Dan tells you "he needs your car an extra day to track down the leak."

Ken requested an estimate. Dan told him it would cost at most $300, which would be the cost of standard maintenance. He left his car.

I repeated, "Do not leave your car overnight with Dan and do not let him take your car apart or he will, very likely, find a leak in the middle of your car's engine."

Despite my warnings, Ken left his car overnight and Dan found a leak in the middle of his car's engine. It was only an $8 part that needed to be replaced, but it took 8 hours of additional labor to repair. Because Dan "liked him," he only charged him for 6 hours or another $450.

Ken announced that he had "learned his lesson." I was dumbfounded.

The ability to learn from our own mistakes or experiences is a fundamental skill that enables us to continuously improve ourselves.

In Japan, home of some of the most proficient manufacturing companies in the world, the principle of continuous improvement is called Kaizen. Problems or defects are identified at the earliest possible stage and corrective actions are taken immediately. These improvements became a formal part of the new system. Toyota used this principle as the core of its production system to become a global powerhouse.

Similarly, we can use this principle to improve our own lives and ensure that every setback or mistake can be used for learning.

From my experience with Dan, I learned not to trust him and to require a written estimate before allowing anyone to fix my car.

More importantly, I was reminded to follow my intuition. As I reflected on this point, I realized that my greatest mistakes in life have all come from failing to follow my intuition. The ability to think logically is one of mankind's greatest gifts, but if it ever contradicts your intuition, learn from my mistake, and FIND OUT WHY. When logic and intuition mesh, then you can be reasonably assured you're on the right track. If not, then gather more information.

If you pay attention, you can also learn from other people's experiences. Ken, obviously, did not learn from my misfortune. He chose to disregard what happened and suffered for it. It can be very painful to watch people, especially those close to you, sabotage themselves. Even so, it is critical to remain detached and let them make their own mistakes (and hopefully learn from them). This is another lesson Ken taught me.

When your mind is open and you approach every experience as an opportunity to learn, even a "less-than-honest" car mechanic can teach you valuable lessons.

44

Habit

Depending on the level of conscious awareness you invest in a habit's creation, habits can either enslave you, turning you into a mindless automaton, or free you to pursue creative, joyful activities that enhance and give meaning to your life.

"Man is a creature of habit."

This simple statement is deceptively profound. Most people's lives are comprised of a collection of habits that dictate many of their physical, emotional and mental actions and reactions. Depending on the level of conscious awareness you invest in a habit's creation, habits can either enslave you, turning you into a mindless automaton, or free you to pursue creative, joyful activities that enhance and give meaning to your life. Most people have a mixture of good and bad habits.

Habit is defined as an acquired behavior pattern followed until it has become almost involuntary. Habits can be good or bad, productive or non-productive. Good habits lead to skills, such as learning to ride a bicycle. They also save you time and energy by automating the performance of desirable actions. Brushing your teeth or driving a car are examples. These acquired behavior patterns free your mind from having to concentrate, as would be required of unfamiliar actions.

Bad habits predispose you to undesirable outcomes. Excessive drinking, smoking, drug use and overeating are examples of bad habits that can harm your body and impair your judgment, aside from wasting your time.

Common sense tells us that you want to replace bad habits with good ones, which is the basis of all self-development and evolution. But as almost everyone who has ever tried to quit smoking will tell you, this is not always as easy as it would seem.

Smokers are addicted to nicotine. But according to modern brain science, all habits induce emotional states that produce chemicals in your brain. Consequently, you become addicted to the chemicals secreted by your brain no matter what kind of habit you create!

With every thought or action you undertake, you create electrical pathways in your brain. As Joseph Dispenza says in the movie **What the Bleep do We Know?,** "neurons which fire together, wire together." Repetition etches these patterns more deeply into your brain.

To replace a bad habit with a good one, you need to break the association with your emotions and the chemicals you've grown accustomed to, and rewire your brain. This requires concentration and will.

If you are unaware or unwilling to acknowledge your non-productive habit, you will have a hard time replacing it. If you are not convinced a particular habit is bad for you, you will have no incentive to change it. But, if you are aware of your unwanted habit and are willing to devote your attention to it, then it can be changed. Deeply focused concentration, such as during a visualization exercise, increases the potency of your thoughts and more deeply affects your brain's rewiring.

Remember, it took regular action to install your unwanted habit—possibly over the course of several lifetimes—so it will take regular action to undo it. This is where your will comes in.

You strengthen your will, as well as your habit, with repetition. Every time you consciously reject the urge to give in to your bad habit, you strengthen your will. Every time you consciously undertake an action to install a new, positive habit, it becomes easier. This is how you rewire your brain and overcome your addictions.

When these habits are of a positive nature, this self-reinforcing cycle produces positive results, but the contrary is also true. This demonstrates a principle that Jesus taught, "For he that hath, to him shall be given; and he that hath not, from him shall be taken even that which he hath."

In other words, consciously acting to install positive habits strengthens your will and further attracts more like experiences. Giving in to bad habits, weakens your will, not only making it harder to install good habits, but doing so may cause you to lose what good habits you already had.

Can there be any better reason to develop your will and consciously establish positive habits?

The development of good habits is meant to improve your life, free you from the grip of negative habits and attract even more positive experiences to you. At the same time, always remember to be guided by wisdom and not convention. You should strive to perform good actions based on your own inner wisdom and conscious choice, not based on convention—not even good habits. This is the ultimate freedom.

45

Don't Follow Your Instincts

"Follow your instincts" seems like good advice. But blindly following your instincts can actually be a surefire recipe for disaster and set back your spiritual development.

"Follow your instincts" seems like good advice. After all, it seems like the "natural" thing to do. And this is especially true when it's contrasted with following some tortured, overly-analyzed intellectual reasoning, which may or may not make sense. But blindly following your instincts can actually be a surefire recipe for disaster **and** set back your spiritual development.

Many people confuse instinct with intuition, but they are actually two different things.

The dictionary defines instinct as:

1. An inborn pattern of behavior that is characteristic of a species and is often a response to specific environmental stimuli.
2. A powerful motivation or impulse.

While, intuition is defined as:

1. The act or faculty of knowing or sensing without the use of rational processes; immediate cognition.
2. Instinctive knowing.

This particular dictionary uses the term instinct to define intuition, so it's no wonder people are confused! Both instinct and intuition involve impulses that originate from outside the conscious mind. ***What distinguishes one from the other is the source of the impulse.***

Your mind operates at three different levels: intellectual, instinctive and intuitive. These levels overlap with one another, but are essentially separate.

Your intellectual or conscious mind is used to perform logical problem-solving activities. This is where you exercise your will, with input from your senses and other levels of your mind.

The instinctive mind is responsible for running your body's autonomic nervous system, which regulates your heart-beat, fills your lungs with air, and sends blood throughout your body. Obviously, these functions are vitally important to your health and you'd never want to interfere with their smooth operation. In fact, using your intellectual mind to override your instinctive mind can put your body into disharmony, leading to stress and disease. But this does not mean you should ***follow*** your instincts!

Your instinctive mind is also responsible for the fight or flight response and the urge to procreate. Can you imagine what our world would be like if we just took whatever object we desired, beat up anyone who disagreed with us, or copulated with anyone without regard to the consequences? Well, the world we live in today often looks like that kind of world! And that's not a good thing!

As human beings, we possess self-awareness, which distinguishes us from animals. But our animal instincts (fight or flight, urge to procreate, etc.) still exist within us. They are our heritage, and represent thoughts that were important for survival at one stage in our species' evolution. But they are ***not*** necessarily helpful to our ***spiritual*** evolution. It is up to you to choose to exercise your will and master these impulses, with input from your intuition.

Your intuition is your inner master or higher self attempting to communicate with you. This is what is responsible for creative breakthroughs and insights, which propel our human race forward. Intuition is altruistic and loving, and, in the mystic's worldview, that which leads to peace, bliss and Oneness.

Several years ago, I got an opportunity to tap into each aspect of my mind in their purest forms. I was visiting a tiger sanctuary in the Everglades, west of Miami. The curator was caring for several subspecies of endangered tigers, which were used for breeding purposes to help the animals regain their numbers. Tigers are the largest cats on earth, and the golden tiger is the largest subspecies.

These wild animals were kept in large pens with 18-foot tall chain link fences. Sanctuary rules prohibited children from the grounds, as the tigers viewed small children as food. During my visit there, I saw the curator send one couple and their infant son away for this reason.

While I was relaxing in the shade of a tree, without warning, a wave of primal emotion swept over me that jolted me to instant alertness. My instinctive mind was silently yelling, "Danger!" Looking up, I saw, about 50 feet away, a huge tiger laying motionless atop an eight-foot perch in the middle of his pen. His eyes were transfixed at what seemed to be me!

I heard the shuffling of feet behind me. The same couple who had been sent away earlier walked past me carrying their infant son towards the tiger.

As soon as they stopped near the fence, the tiger leaped off his perch and fully splayed himself against the chain link fence on his hind legs, tantalized by the "morsel of food" just out of his reach.

The tiger watched as the furious curator threw the not-too-bright parents and their child off the grounds.

Intellectually, I knew I was not in any danger. As I stood there, suddenly, I wanted to feel what the tiger was feeling. Slowly, I began walking towards the tiger.

The tiger ignored me until the child was out of sight. Then, he dropped down on his four legs and began to stare at me.

I looked into his eyes and communicated the thought, "I am like you." He walked towards me and began pacing back and forth, his eyes locked onto mine, with just a few feet and the chain link fence separating us. He was truly an impressively beast, his exotically striped head being the width of my chest. I continued to tell him, "I am like you."

Still staring at me, in mid-stride, he stopped right in front of me, then laid down at my feet, like a dog. I crouched down to get closer. He closed his eyes and went to sleep.

The curator returned to see that his tiger was not only calm, but had made a new friend.

In this encounter I got to sense: 1) my instinctive mind warn me of possible danger; 2) my intellectual mind reason that I was actually *not* in danger; and 3) my intuitive mind inspire me to let myself commune or energetically merge with the tiger.

So it is in everyday life. When you receive an "impulse" from outside of your conscious mind, ask yourself if it's an instinct or your intuition. Is it based on the remnants of an urge for survival ... or is it the drive toward Oneness? The more you listen to your intuition and take action based on *it*, the faster your life and the world will transform for the better. After all, your intuition is the voice of your higher self; the entire universe will work with you to make its unique song heard.

So, don't follow your instincts ... follow your intuition!

46

The Myth of Multitasking

There are two aspects of computers that can help us to understand how the conscious mind works and how we can be more efficient, but remember: multitasking is a myth.

Last week, a discussion thread on a University of Chicago Business School online forum asked the question, "Are we getting anywhere with multitasking?"

Many companies are attempting to keep labor costs low by asking employees to perform several tasks at once. Even if you're not in business, you may frequently be tempted to try and multitask. For example, you might try cooking dinner while studying or checking your email. In other words, you try to "do" more than one thing at a time, in order to "be more efficient and effective." ***But is that really what you're doing?***

The analogy for today's compulsive drive to multitask is the computer, which seemingly performs several functions at the same time. In reality, no single processor (CPU) can multitask, nor can a human. Multitasking, as it is commonly presented, is a myth.

Computers seemingly multitask by dividing the time they spend processing data into tiny slices, much smaller than a second. They perform one task exclusively for that tiny time slice and then switch to another task, which they perform exclusively, before switching again. To the outsider, it looks like the computer is performing several tasks at once; but that's not the case.

Computer designers get around this limitation by using more than one processor. (The Intel Core2 Duo is an example.) These parallel processing computers use several CPUs to process data at the same time. This is not multitasking, but rather multiprocessing. It is akin to getting help from outside parties ...

and is actually a powerful problem-solver, one that we can exploit as humans—even if we don't have a staff of office workers or housekeepers to serve us.

Computers have two characteristics that mimic the actions of the conscious mind:

Focusing

Just like a computer, for any activity that requires our conscious mind, we are most effective when focusing on one task at a time. Any time we divide our attention, we are prone to making mistakes. Think of the last time you spilled something. Likely, it's because you were focused on something else. How many times have you seen a football player drop a pass because he's already thinking about where to run before he's caught the ball?

Focusing is critical to completing any task effectively. Keeping a single objective in sharp focus also avoids the "spinning your wheels—switching from task to task and not getting anything done" state of mind ... which is why computers will sometimes "hang." When this happens to you, just like a computer, you need to shut down all extra tasks (windows) and start over (reboot), focusing on your primary objective.

Some people might argue that multitasking is what enables us to "walk and chew gum" at the same time. This is an example of two behaviors that no longer require our conscious mind to execute. By repetition, you have effectively "delegated" your walking and chewing gum activities to a lower level of the conscious mind, the level of habit.

Examples of habits are driving or riding a bicycle. In most instances, either can be undertaken without the need for your conscious mind's participation. That's why people often talk on their cell phones while driving. The danger comes when the unexpected occurs and thinking is required. If the conscious mind is preoccupied with a conversation, it won't be able to devote its full processing power to the task at hand, and you're more likely to get into an accident.

Delegating

Delegating routine tasks to the level of habit can "free up your conscious mind," but you still risk accidents; because habit is still a conscious activity. A better way is to ask for help from other aspects of your mind that are not conscious: your subconscious or superconscious mind.

As was described in the last chapter, *Don't Follow Your Instincts*, your mind can be divided into three levels: conscious, instinctive/subconscious and intuitive/superconscious.

In order to complete a project in the business world, as a manager, you would delegate various tasks to your subordinates. In the household, you would delegate appropriate tasks to your housekeepers. If you don't have these resources available, you can still get help.

Many people do this "instinctively" by thinking about a problem and then "sleeping on it." What they have done is informally delegated the task to their subconscious and/or superconscious minds. You can do the same by formally asking them for help.

The easiest technique is to ask just before you go to sleep. Your subconscious mind will work on the task you assign it, without question or complaint. Your intuitive mind may also help, especially if it is regularly helping with your spiritual advancement (e.g., if you're practicing meditation or consciously using your intuition on a daily basis).

The trick to getting results is to write down or record your impressions as soon as you wake up—just as if you were journaling your dreams. Write down your thoughts, even if they don't make sense, before you get distracted with the mundane affairs of the day (such as eating or preparing for work).

Later, when you're able to devote your full conscious attention to the task you delegated, you can look at your earlier notes and reflect on them. You may be amazed at the insights you have come up with and possible solutions. It is often a simple matter to identify the job your subconscious and intui-tion has done for you.

Conclusion

When you are faced with several tasks that need to be done in short order, remember to ask for help—especially from your subconscious and superconscious mind—and focus solely on one task at a time. You'll be more productive and less accident prone. Don't try multitasking—it's a myth.

47

The Path Toward Oneness

Within each of us, there exists an inner compass or soul urge that is driving us back to Oneness. It manifests in many different ways—even in times of war.

Last week, while flying from Virginia back to Florida, I sat next to a young man. He was wearing civilian clothes, but I overheard him mention he was on leave from Afghanistan.

He was smiling, happy and completely relaxed. Even recognizing that he would **naturally** be relieved to be getting a little R&R, I was struck by how completely at ease and at peace he was. I asked him if he was this relaxed back in Afghanistan.

He laughed and said, "Not quite. We're in a valley near the Pakistan border and every day someone is firing shots or launching mortars at us."

He was bright, clear eyed and open minded. He was teaching himself the Pashto language so he could talk with the villagers. He had an understanding of the situation on the ground that came from direct experience, not the misinfor-mation you get from some biased political account.

When I mentioned that I wrote a book that takes place, in part, in Pakistan he was intrigued. When I told him the characters were practicing advanced mystic skills like telepathy, remote viewing and astral projection, he was at rapt attention.

He told me he was raised as a Christian but accepted that everyone should be free to practice whatever religion they chose. He asked me all sorts of questions about mysticism and my concept of God. He was a sponge for information.

I explained that everyone is free to form their own conception of God, but in the mystic view all is One. Most religions, at their core, profess that God is omnipresent, omnipotent and omniscient, that is, all present, all powerful and all knowing.

The only way that God could have these three attributes is if God is One. Otherwise God would not be omnipresent. There cannot be anything outside of the One, because what could possibly divide the One?

He took my words in scientifically and without judgment, gathering information and weighing it carefully before forming any conclusions. He was acting like a true mystic.

I continued. Our entire universe exists solely in the One, or in other words, in the mind of God. Again, our universe cannot exist outside of the One, for then the One would not be omnipresent.

Within each one of us, there exists a Divine aspect, which animates us. This is our soul. God is in each of us.

I offered an analogy. As the author of **Mystic Warrior**, I created an entire universe. I am the "God of that universe." It exists in my mind and one of the characters, Alec Thorn, also exists in my mind. *He is in me*.

Conversely, I gave birth to Alec Thorn. He now has an existence independent of me. People who "get to know him" by reading **Mystic Warrior** could predict how he would react in different scenarios. While he is not me, I am the animating force that gives him life. *I am in him*.

One of Jesus' most famous quotes about the Father can now be understood. When he says, *"He is in me and I am in Him,"* he is stating a universal truth—one which is true for every man, woman and child on earth.

If you stop and contemplate this, you will come to realize that *the soul within each of us is the same soul*. Every one of us is animated by this same Divine aspect. We are each single points of awareness in the One.

Here on earth, we clothe our true nature with physical, emotional, mental and spiritual bodies which are formed from our choices and experiences over lifetimes. It is our soul personality, not our actual soul, which creates the illusion of separation.

Within us, there exists an inner compass or soul urge that is driving us back to Oneness. The path towards Oneness consists of embracing higher vibrational energies that lead to love, peace, joy and unity and discarding the lower vibrational ones that lead to fear, anger, hatred and separation.

Our purpose in life is to attune with God, to listen to the Divine aspect or inner master in the heart of each of us and to follow the guidance within. By doing so, we will naturally discard false beliefs and move towards unity.

As we began our descent, the young man nodded and said, "Very interesting. You've given me a lot to think about."

Then I recognized that in his own way, this young man was already doing exactly what I had described. His learning a foreign language and communicating directly with the villagers of Afghanistan was forming a bridge. He was listening to his inner master and furthering our progress on the path towards Oneness.

48

When the Student is Ready...

When the student is ready the teacher will appear; when the student is sufficiently advanced, the teacher may disappear.

In October, I was on the Ascension Panel at the **Conscious Life Expo** in Los Angeles. I offered to give everyone who stopped by our booth later that day a "hit of energy" so they would feel what higher vibrational energy was like.

Close to a hundred people took me up on my offer. Most of them signed up for my free series of lessons and I sold all the copies of my book, **Mystic Warrior**, my **Energy Center Clearing** package and my **Total Love Immersion** CD that I had. It was a great day for everyone.

A few weeks later, a reader wrote to tell me how much she enjoyed meeting me at the expo and reading the lessons, which she described as "amazing." Then she told me that she had me "looked at" by her energy healer.

Her healer told her that there was negativity connected with my energy path. She made it clear that she would not purchase any of my products, unless I could "win over" her healer.

I wrote back that one of the primary lessons that any true mystic teaches is to listen to your own inner master. While it's often valuable to solicit outside advice, your ultimate source of wisdom lies within. I told her that if she enjoyed the energy boost and found my lessons "amazing," she would likely appreciate my books and CDs, but that she would have to decide on her own. I was not going to "negotiate" with her teacher.

This is not the first time I have come across a student who has come to over rely on his or her teacher. In some cases, I've watched as students, far more gifted than their teachers, gave away their power to them and let them direct every aspect of their lives.

In one extreme case, I listened to a "teacher" complain, "The hotel people can't do anything right," "I'm not getting any support from my staff," and then yell at her assistant for not waking her up when she had "obviously overslept."

I explained to her, "You get more of whatever you complain about." She was disempowering her students and training them to be victims. My words fell on deaf ears. As Dan Kennedy, a popular direct marketer, once said, "Most people are running around with their umbilical cords in their hands looking for another place to plug it in." Relying on anyone to direct your life is contrary to the mystic path that I was taught.

My first mentor, "Sophie," made this exceedingly clear to me. She is a true master who "chooses" her students when she deems them worthy and ready. You cannot buy her services at any price or even find her, unless she decides to be found. My earnestness attracted her attention. She opened me up energetically and advised me on numerous subjects.

You can imagine how lucky I felt to have such advice. But as soon as she decided I was at the level where I should be "self-sufficient," she disappeared, leaving no forwarding address or phone. I couldn't even connect with her in my meditations. The message to me was painful, but clear: do not become reliant on any source of wisdom, other than your own inner master.

Krishnamurti was another master who did something even more dramatic. At the height of his popularity, when he had thousands of devoted followers, he disbanded his organization. He wrote a beautiful, open letter to them all, in which he explained that he didn't want his followers to become reliant upon him.

A few years ago, while on a tour of Tibet, I met two Buddhist monks, who had been monks for 8 and 14 years, respectively. During our final dinner, I decided to celebrate by drinking a local Tibet Green Barley Beer. The less experienced monk told me, via a translator, that my violation of the law against drinking alcohol had me headed for a future life as a dog.

I laughed and politely disagreed with him, arguing that all laws must be interpreted spiritually, that there was no absolute rule in this area. The ultimate master lies within. The more experienced monk agreed with me and added that it was one of the most difficult lessons that new monks must master.

To her credit, my new reader emailed me to say she is trying to reconcile the advice of her "infallible" teacher and what she experienced.

Most people give up and leave the dissonance to fester in their mind, unresolved and awaiting a new, more painful trigger, one which will eventually force them to deal with the issue. She is persistent, however. If she goes within and contemplates her situation, she may come to an acceptable resolution. Hopefully, she will choose to rely on her own inner master.

As a corollary, since I'm the one who introduced the dissonance and "forced" her to think, she may throw away both me and my teachings. However, that is not my concern. Throughout history, people are famous for "shooting the messenger," i.e., deriding the bearer of bad news.

In my view, the role of the teacher is to inspire their students to go within, seek answers themselves and become self-sufficient.

It occurs to me: when the student is ready the teacher will appear; when the student is sufficiently advanced, the teacher may disappear.

49

The Path is Seldom Straight

In our instant-gratification society, whether it's health, wealth or love, we have been conditioned to expect that anything we desire will be obtained in short order. The mystic path is seldom straight.

Many years ago, a long term mystic told me I reminded him of a "rosebud."

It didn't seem very flattering to me at the time. In my view, I was progressing very rapidly on my spiritual path and "rosebud" seemed to imply "beginner." I expected to be a full-blown master very soon.

Of course, he was right.

In our instant-gratification society, we have been conditioned to expect that anything we desire will be obtained in short order. If you're feeling uncomfortable, you're taught to take a drug to banish the discomfort. If you desire better health, greater wealth or more love, you are instructed to sign up for a special program (requiring no prior training and no effort) and you will obtain it straight away.

The mystic path is seldom straight.

Even in the face of earnest intentions, sincere dedication and adherence to universal spiritual principles, there may come times when it appears you are *just not making any progress*. Sometimes, you may even feel like you're regressing!

What I have learned has clearly demonstrated one truth about such times—they're normal.

The knowledge and experiences that you (your ego and your higher self) are manifesting in this physical world must be embraced, contemplated, understood and become a part of your being *before* they will be transmuted into mystic virtues like wisdom, humility and compassion.

And if you wonder, "Why bother?" you can rest assured these mystic virtues will be held in reserve and made available to you, *when you need them*.

To an outside observer, and perhaps sometimes to you, the process of assimilating these experiences may look like stagnation.

It's analogous to what elementary science students observe when they're asked to heat an ice cube and take temperature readings. Students watch the temperature rise steadily with the application of heat, but are puzzled when the temperature plateaus at 32 degrees F (0 degrees C). Most students expect the temperature to continue rising steadily upward, but it will not resume its upward trend until all the ice has melted.

So it is for the student of mysticism. There will be plateaus. There will also be *apparent* setbacks.

Oftentimes, a setback will occur immediately after a breakthrough.

This is also commonplace. Subconsciously, you may invite conflict into your life, as a way for you to demonstrate mastery of the subject. When you can face your adversaries and succeed (both internally and externally), you will have further embodied the lessons into your being.

Neither should you be afraid of asking for help.

All the avatars who founded our major religions received guidance and teachings from mystic masters. No one was born "enlightened," nor did anyone go from illiteracy to enlightenment in a single incident. And while such self-illumination may have arrived while sitting under a Bodhi tree, it was not the result of one particular action (or inaction), but the accumula-tion of numerous prior experiences and teachings, sometimes over lifetimes.

It is the nature of learning to fail. The biggest winners are those who fail the most, yet who steadfastly keep trying. The same applies to spiritual growth.

Everyone must be allowed to fail.

At some point, there may come a time when you feel you have progressed. There is no need to "announce" your new-found mastery to the world. This is your ego attempting to regain control of your spiritual progress.

It's similar to an entrepreneur who may be the epitome of humility and open-mindedness while he is busy trying to raise capital, but who suddenly considers himself a "genius" when funds appear in the company's coffers and the hint of success appears on the horizon.

It is unnecessary. Better to lead by example.

Whether you are steadily growing, plateauing, regressing or making a quantum leap, remember that the essential YOU has never changed. The process of enlightenment is the gradual unfolding of that true, inner YOU, so that the outer you reflects the magnificent being you are.

This process is symbolized by the rose in the west and the lotus in the east. It is the gradual unfolding of the soul to reveal the intrinsic beauty contained within.

So whatever your spiritual tradition, whatever your stage on the path, you are destined to be a beautiful flower in the garden of the universe.

And don't be offended, if someone calls you a "rosebud!"

50

Never Offer to Rid a Man of his Demons

Unless you're absolutely sure of a person's intention, as a word of caution, never offer to rid a man of his demons.

The other day a man cursed me—up, down and sideways—with some of the most colorful expletives I've ever heard, for five minutes straight! In retrospect, I should have expected it—I had offered to get rid of his demons.

You might think that offering to help someone would always be welcomed, especially if they first request it. But no, not always. It's useful to be absolutely sure before you walk into such a potential mine field.

Last Friday, I was relaxing with my friend, Bobby, enjoying a delightful pale ale at a local restaurant. I was describing my upcoming event where I would show people how to clear out their energy centers to relieve stress and feel light, free and energized.

That was when Bobby's friend John walked up. Bobby introduced us and John seemed interested in the energy work that I was describing. As soon as Bobby walked over to talk to some other friends he recognized, John had my full attention.

John was a medium-sized man with a fluffy, white beard. He seemed very pleasant, but even in the dim light, I could see pain in his eyes.

He asked what my event would do for him, if he were to attend. I told him it would get rid of discordant energies surrounding him and he would "bliss out."

That's when he leaned a little closer and asked, "How much would it cost to get rid of my demons?"

I said, "Twenty bucks. Just come on Wednesday and I'll make sure they're gone."

He said, "For 20 bucks, you can get rid of my demons?"
I nodded, "Yes."

That's when he exploded. He told me there was no way I could get rid of his demons. That I was a quack, a charlatan and a thief, preying on gullible people.

I assumed that he had misunderstood me.

I said, "I can get rid of your discordant energies, including your negative thoughts, feeling your negative feelings and doing your negative acts, your demons will come back."

He ignored me and continued his expletive-filled tirade.

While he paused for breath, I explained further, "Jesus healed lots of people. Do you remember what he would say afterwards? Go and sin no more."

I leaned closer to try and get him to focus on what I was saying, rather than sit back while he remained stuck in his anger. "Do you understand what he meant? It wasn't a moral judgment. He was just telling people that after he healed them, not to go back to doing the same unhealthy things that got them sick in the first place."

Reason was no longer working with John. His stream of colorful (and uncommon) curse words continued.

I tried to agree with John.

"You're right. I can't get rid of your demons."

He continued his rant. I came to a realization and decided to share it.

"I can't get rid of your demons, because you're too attached to them."

What part of John's face that was not covered by his beard got even redder, while he continued screaming even louder, incoherently, and completely out of control.

I did not sense any physical danger. John was not the type who beat people up—more likely, he was the type who got beaten up, which would add to his tales of woe and add to his list of demons he could complain about.

Finally, I had enough. I said, "Forget it. My offer is withdrawn. Just continue on with your life, just as it is."

Before John could react, Bobby rushed over. He put his hand on John's shoulder and asked him several times to "calm down and relax," reminding him, "Ed is a very good friend of mine."

As if a light switch was turned off, John abruptly stopped and apologized to me.

I shook his hand and said, "Apology accepted."

Then John stepped back, took a deep breath and walked out the door.

Bobby shrugged and said, "Underneath it all, he's actually a nice guy."

And I realized, so is almost everyone "a nice person, underneath it all." It's only when we get attached to our own image of who we are that things can get off track.

It doesn't matter if that perceived image is one full of virtue or one filled with demons. If you threaten someone's self-image, he or she will rebel. And when you threaten to "take down" their self-image (by offering to rid a person of his demons, for example), you risk having that someone fight you for what they presume to be "who they are."

The point is that we are not our perceived demons *or* our perceived virtues. We are majestic spiritual beings living a human life. Ultimately, we are single points of awareness in the Oneness that is Reality. To identify with such superficial attributes is not in tune with our true nature and will lead to needless conflict.

But while we continue to grow, evolve and approach these higher states of consciousness, unless you're absolutely sure of a person's intention, as a word of caution, never offer to rid a man of his demons.

51

5 Thoughts on Helping Others

Your entire mission as a majestic spiritual being incarnate on earth is to tap into your inner- most self and radiate your wisdom, love and energy to the universe. Your ability to help others is related in large part to how connected you are to your innermost self.

If you are reading this chapter, it's likely you earn your livelihood by helping others. And even if you are not formally doing this as a profession, it's likely you are often called upon to give aid and advice to family, friends, co-workers and/or loved ones. It is our nature to want to help others, especially those who are suffering.

As I've written before, your entire mission as a majestic spiritual being, temporarily incarnated here on earth, is to tap into your innermost self and radiate your wisdom, love and energy to the universe. Your ability to help those in need is related, in large part, to how well connected you are to your innermost self.

The late Indian sage, Nisargadatta Maharaj, based his entire philosophy of helping others around his teaching that, "knowing who you truly are" is the single most important thing you can do to help anyone and consequently the world.

Here are a few of his thoughts on help, taken from his classic book, *I Am That*, along with both my headings and comments:

Help so that someone no longer needs your help.

> *"The only help worth giving is freeing from the need for further help. Repeated help is no help at all. Do not talk of helping another, unless you can put him beyond all need of help."*

This is akin to the proverb, "Give a man a fish, you feed him for a day. Teach a man to fish, you feed him for a lifetime." Teaching someone a skill puts that person beyond the need for further help.

Help by setting a good example.

> *"You can help another by your precept and example and, above all, by your being. You cannot give what you do not have."*

The best teacher is someone who leads by example. As Gandhi said, "Be the change you want to see in the world." However, if you do not ***already*** embody the help you wish to offer, it might be wise to hold off on the helping, since you would not actually be in a position to help, and focus your attention, instead, on the "becoming." That is, "becoming" the person who *is* in position to help.

Do not attempt to help when you are emotionally attached to the outcome.

> *"If you really want to help a person, keep away. If you are emotionally committed to helping, you will fail to help."*

Your emotional commitment to "helping" sends out an energy that will attract people to you who will satisfy your craving—that is, they'll need help! The problem is, this may merely set up a codependent relationship, one that inordinately pulls at you, confounds you and drains you, with typically little to show in the way of positive change on the part of the one being "helped."

Your most effective advice comes when you have a detached interest in the outcome. Some will mistake this detachment for "not caring;" but when your intention is pure, it is the highest form of help you can offer. Please note: sending love, even from afar, can always be used to help others in need.

Help in those areas where you already have what they need.

> "Ceasing to do evil precedes beginning to do good. Of course, if you have a chance to help somebody, by all means do it and promptly too; don't keep him waiting 'til you are perfect."

As a long-term mystic once counseled me, "We are all students on the path. Some who are farther along the path may be called upon to help you; others, who have not traveled as far, may look to you for help." Consequently, offer aid to those who ask in those areas where you already have what they need.

The most important help you can offer comes from knowing who you are.

> "There is nothing that can help the world more than your putting an end to ignorance. Then you need not do anything in particular to help the world. Your very being is a help, action or no action."
>
> "First be free of suffering yourself and then only hope of helping others. Your very existence will be the greatest help a man can give to his fellow man."
>
> "There are people in the world who do more good than all the statesmen and philanthropists put together. They radiate light and peace with no intention or knowledge."

In the above quotations, the ignorance Nisargadatta refers to is the ignorance of who you truly are ... and suffering is the result of this ignorance. When you know and embody the truth of who you really are, you are in a position to do the most good possible for yourself, others and the world.

It goes without saying, but a final adage is: "Don't offer unsolicited help." This tendency is usually tied to having an emotional attachment to the outcome. A word of caution: it can backfire miserably, even when someone does ask for it, as I wrote in the last chapter, *Never Offer to Rid a Man of His Demons*.

A final Nisargadatta quotation, which sums up his philosophy and which points to the state that we all seek to embody:

> *"If you want to help the world, you must be beyond the need of help. Then, all your doing, as well as not doing, will help the world most effectively."*

We all seek to be self-realized, to know who we truly are. This is our most important "mission on earth" and represents the ultimate gift we can offer to the world.

52

The Power of Presence

Practicing Presence is powerful. It transcends time, amplifies your thoughts and emotions, and naturally induces feelings of gratitude.

Last month, a Canadian reader emailed me about an experience that beautifully illustrates the benefits of cultivating an appreciation for living in the moment, or what I like to call, the "Power of Presence."

> *Hi Ed,*
> *It has been just over a week since the energy clearing session with you. As the day went on, I noticed my lower back wasn't aching. My lower back had been causing me a lot of pain in the previous weeks. And it still feels good, which is wonderful. I do feel I should tell you about what happened later that morning.*
> *I drove to work just after the session; I care for a wonderful 90-year old man with a mind as sharp as a tack. It turned out to be a beautiful morning and I suggested to Roy that we sit out on his sundeck in the sunshine.*
> *His deck is high up on the main floor of his two-story house which is on a hill, the view is spectacular. From the deck we could look down at the lake with the mountains behind that. Everything looked so sharp that morning, the sky was so blue and the clouds were so white, the lake was a darker green than the mountains behind it. It was a gorgeous morning and incredibly quiet.*

I commented to Roy I felt like I was waiting for the show to start, it was so still and very quiet—like the hush that happens just before the curtain opens at a play. The words barely came out of my mouth when two massive bald eagles swooped into the sky directly up in front of us.

They were facing one another, colliding together for a moment; they were screeching at each other, they were absolutely magnificent and their wing span was just massive. I could see every feather and detail; one eagle had a white head and tail feathers and the other one was more mottled. They were breathtaking, huge, majestic and so strong.

They parted, flew into the nearby trees. Each eagle sat on a separate tree for about 10 minutes and as if by some unheard signal they flew up in unison, wing to wing and soared past the trees down to the lake.

Now it is true eagles live here and they are my all time favorite bird, but I have never witnessed this before! Maybe it was a coincidence and I would have seen it anyway but I am not so sure.

I have appreciated that view for a long time but the difference was probably the unusual feeling of calm, quiet and tranquility inside of me at that moment. I was really in that moment, with no other mind chatter going on. The thought that came to me while I was feeling like that this must be the peace that the creative force, or Source or God operates from. To me it was amazing.

Thanks a lot,
Cindy
Vancouver Island, Canada

Presence is a state of being in which you're naturally placing your full awareness on what you are experiencing in the "now"; you are in sync with your higher self; and your thoughts of past or future events have disappeared, leaving you to just "be" with what or who is before you.

When you are Present, synchronicities are commonplace, as you are tapping into the Oneness, where everything is connected. You are in a state of being where you recognize that ***everything is a synchronicity***.

Presence amplifies your thoughts and feelings, because you have incorporated more of your entire being into your experience. You are no longer limited to the power of your intellect.

Presence leads to joy and fun. Conversely, the inability to have fun is almost always tied to a lack of Presence. Witness the boorish behavior often seen in public, where people are talking or texting on their cell phones, or worrying about some past or future event, versus focusing their attention on their present companion. How often do these people look joyful?

Presence enhances Intimacy. If you want to be intimate with another person, you, obviously, need to spend time with them. But "spending time with them" is not enough. For true intimacy, you need to be Present during that time you spend together, i.e., what is popularly called "quality time."

Conversely, if you preface your visit with "warnings" that you may have to take a phone call or leave to attend a "more important" meeting, you already have one foot out the door. You are denying yourself and your companion the joy that comes with sharing Presence.

So, the next time you are "bored," rather than look outside of yourself for something to stimulate your mind, embrace your experience by placing your full awareness on what's happening. Focus your attention on an aspect of the situation that you appreciate.

By embracing your experience, you will become more Present. You will naturally radiate gratitude. The universe will respond by giving you more of what you appreciate, for you are "shouting" to the universe, "Give me more of this!" with a megaphone that is sure to produce inner and outer results.

Practicing Presence is powerful. It transcends time, with the potential to change your life. Try it out and let me know what happens—especially if any eagles show up.

UPDATE: Here's an update that Cindy emailed a few weeks later:

> *Hi Ed,*
> *Yesterday, Roy and I were again sitting on his deck. Some humming birds were flitting in and out of the hanging baskets, so I started aiming my camera. They are hard to photograph because they move incredibly fast, but yesterday ... it was like they were posing for me,* ***every picture I took came out beautifully!***

http://MysticWarrior.us/images/hummingbird_by_cindy.jpg

> *I caught them in flight with their wings backward, forwards; hovering every which way. They don't usually hang around that long. I was in the moment then; I just kept clicking, clicking and clicking and at the end I said thank you. It just came out of my mouth.*
> *I have been trying to get pictures like that for years! I was fully concentrating on those humming birds so I was in the moment. I guess that's the "Power of Presence."*
> *Cindy*
> *Vancouver Island, Canada*

There's nothing else to say other than ***Cindy is still living in the moment!***

53

Being in this World, But Not of It

The mystic adage "Be in this world, but not of it" is not meant to imply you should avoid the mundane world, but rather to engage and share your unique gifts with the rest of humanity.

There is a mystic adage that suggests we should strive "to be in this world, but not of it."

This does not imply you should shun this "crude world" for some perceived "higher world," where you may feel you more rightly belong.

All worlds exist simultaneously in the eternal NOW. It is self-deception to state you are waiting for some "higher, better or more enlightened" world where you will be recognized or more fully appreciated. That world exists right here. It is your job to tap into it and live according to the highest principles you can conceive, NOW! By doing so, others will more easily recognize and appreciate you're modeling the essence of this adage.

What this means is that you live, eat, interact, and socialize with the people who comprise this world. Acting to escape or isolate yourself from this world is not the objective. If you want to change the world, you need to engage. "Be the change you wish to see in the world," as Gandhi says.

A friend refers to this as "enlightenment of the marketplace," that is, living in a state in which you are "walking the talk" and embodying these higher truths while participating in the everyday, mundane world.

As the Zen adage states, "Before enlightenment, chop wood, carry water; after enlightenment, chop wood, carry water."

The Rosicrucians are a mystical society that conveys this principle with their symbol—the rose and the cross. The rose is a symbol for the unfolding soul and the cross is symbolic of the human body with arms outstretched. (There is no religious connotation to the cross.) The rose opening on the cross is a metaphor for the soul awakening through the trials and tribulations of physical incarnation.

Mastering the physical world is not always easy. We all regularly find ourselves faced with obstacles and adversity, until we prove our mastery.

It may be comforting to know that these challenges have been arranged by you and your own higher self to compel you to grow mentally and spiritually. When you find yourself outside of your comfort zone, you are actually being given an opportunity to develop capabilities you may not have otherwise discovered.

As Joseph Campbell states, "The cave you fear to enter holds the treasure you seek."

To avoid all conflict is to ensure stagnation.

Do not fear uncertainty or discomfort. Embrace the challenge of being a spiritual being in a world often hallmarked by confusion, where millions of people act in ways contrary to their own best interests. Your job is to do what is right by your highest sense, and in so doing, set an example for others. In this way, they, too, may recognize the truth that all of us are single points of awareness in the Divine Oneness, inspired to act in our own unique ways, but ultimately exemplifying the truth of our Oneness.

"Do not hide your light under a basket," as Jesus taught.

The greatest gift you can share with the world is your recognition of the fact that you are an aspect of the Divine Oneness. Your willingness to share your unique gifts with the world—despite the potential backlash, ridicule, hatred and jealousy—is your contribution to your own spiritual advancement and to the uplifting of humanity. Not with a pious, "know it all" or "above it all" attitude, but by example—by living your truth in the here and now.

Meditation is the primary doorway through which you tap into your innermost essence, your divine aspect, your I AM presence. When you have "gone to the bank" via meditation, then your mission is to spread your "wealth" by interacting with the world.

For the true master not only dwells in the Oneness, but has the skills to apply that enlightenment in the world, to make the path more illumined and accessible to others.

To your success in connecting with your own inner being and sharing it in the world.

Praise for *Mystic Warrior*

*Winner of the Independent Publisher Book Award
for Visionary Fiction*
and
*The Nautilus Silver Book Award
for Fiction/Visionary Fiction*

"*The DaVinci Code* meets *The X-Files*—*Mystic Warrior* takes the spiritual novel to a whole new level. Packed with intrigue, a necessary read for those on the path of adventure."

—**Dannion Brinkley,** *New York Times*
Bestselling author of *Saved by the Light*

"Highly recommended ... deftly written ... *Mystic Warrior* is a twining, suspenseful, and fully unique saga from start to finish."

—*Midwest Book Review*

"This is truly a novel like none other, with much to ponder about what, in the world, is really going on."

—*Magical Blend*

"*Mystic Warrior* is a think-about-it thriller with spiritual truths sprinkled among the action."

—*New Age Retailer*

"Even if you don't believe in psychic powers ... by the end of this book you will seriously be reconsidering the possibility."

—*Hot Lava! Book Reviews*

"The author had me hooked from the first page ... an outstanding grade of modern literature."

—*Roundtable Reviews*

Mystic Warrior

If you enjoyed *Mystic Secrets Revealed*, you may also appreciate *Mystic Warrior: A Novel Beyond Time and Space*...

Alec Thorn is a thirty-something go-getter looking to make it big. When a key business ally dies suspiciously, his dream is shattered. Sophie, an eccentric florist, mysteriously leads him to a discovery that will change his life forever—the leader of an elite group of mercenaries has a personal vendetta against him and wants him dead.

Ominously, the mercenaries are threatening to auction off a nuclear device to fanatic terrorists bent on world destruction. Aided by Sophie and a rogue bounty hunter, Thorn begins a desperate race against time to develop his "spiritual muscles" and survive in a world he had no idea even existed and where his previous beliefs about time and space no longer make sense.

Thorn's spiritual transformation reveals an unknown world of selfless mystics working behind the scenes using advanced psychic abilities to battle terrorists and the power elite. This unassuming entrepreneur-turned-mystic-warrior battles against seemingly insurmountable odds with the fate of millions hanging in the balance.

Mystic Warrior won the *2005 Independent Publisher Book Award Winner for Visionary Fiction* and a *2008 Nautilus Silver Book Award Winner for Fiction/Visionary Fiction*.

For more information, please visit:
http://MysticWarrior.us

Energy Center Clearing

If you would like to relieve stress, calm your mind, increase your energy, and discover how a combination of ancient mystic secrets and modern energy tools, from both East and West, can help you to:

- Connect to your innermost self, more deeply than you might have thought possible …
- Experience a blissful state of lightness and peace—known to mystics as "Peace Profound" …
- Replenish your energy, while balancing and centering yourself …
- Achieve greater clarity and focus …
- Obtain guidance, direction and answers from your own inner master, then please visit:

http://EnergyCenterClearing.com

Here's what people are saying about *Energy Center Clearing*:

"A gift from the higher realms."
—Dr. Raja Merk Dove, StarDoves

"I stopped smoking, after a lifetime of smoking."
—Harriet Forrester, Etowah, NC

"The profound sense of peace that has come over me is beyond anything I have ever experienced before."
—Shen Kahn, London, England

Please visit: **http://EnergyCenterClearing.com**

About the Author

Edwin Harkness Spina is an award-winning author, speaker and mystic. His first book, *Mystic Warrior*, won the *Independent Publisher Book Award for Visionary Fiction* and a *Nautilus Silver Book Award for Fiction*. (Deepak Chopra won the *Nautilus Gold* that year.)

Ed is also a contributing author, along with Zig Ziglar, Brian Tracy, Joe Vitale and others, to the bestseller, *101 Great Ways to Improve Your Life*, the author of *Escaping the Matrix*, and the developer of *Energy Center Clearing* and *Higher Self Integration*.

Prior to shifting his focus to writing and speaking, Ed was a venture capitalist, entrepreneur, software designer and business consultant. He earned an MBA from the University of Chicago and a BSE from Tufts University.

For videos, interviews and more information, please visit:
http://MysticWarrior.us/about

Made in the USA
Middletown, DE
31 March 2024

52359158R00106